A Sustain Me Comprehensive Guide to Herbal Remedies and Natural Healing Inspired by Barbara O'Neill Book

Sustainable Natural Herbal Remedies Healing with Nature's Pharmacy

BY

Barbony O Naill

Contents

Chapter 1: Introduction to Herbal Healing

Understanding the Need for Natural Remedies

In today's world, the prevalence of chronic diseases, mental health challenges, and lifestyle-related conditions has reached alarming levels. Many people are turning to natural remedies as an alternative or complement to conventional medicine. But why? The answer lies in the growing awareness of the side effects of synthetic medications, the rising cost of healthcare, and a collective yearning to reconnect with nature.

This chapter explores the reasons behind the shift toward natural healing. It highlights the limitations of modern medicine, such as its focus on symptom management rather than root-cause healing, and the role of herbal remedies in filling these gaps.

Key points include:

- A historical overview of herbal medicine as humanity's first pharmacy.

- The resurgence of interest in natural healing in the 21st century.

- Testimonials from individuals who have benefited from herbal remedies.

How Barbara O'Neill's Approach Inspires Sustainable Healing

Barbara O'Neill, a renowned natural health educator, has inspired countless individuals to embrace herbal remedies and holistic healing practices. Her teachings emphasize the importance of treating the body as a whole and harnessing the healing power of nature.

In this section, we discuss:

- Barbara O'Neill's philosophy on natural health.

- Her emphasis on lifestyle changes, proper nutrition, and the use of herbs to restore balance.

- Key lessons from her work that have shaped the foundation of this book.

Barbara's message is clear: the body has an incredible ability to heal itself when given the right tools. By integrating sustainable practices with natural remedies, we not only improve our health but also contribute to the well-being of the planet.

What This Book Will Teach You

The purpose of this book is to provide readers with a comprehensive guide to herbal remedies and natural healing, inspired by Barbara O'Neill's teachings. This chapter outlines the journey you'll embark on as you explore the art and science of sustainable herbal medicine.

You'll learn:

- The basics of herbal medicine and its benefits.

- How to grow, harvest, and prepare your own remedies.

- Sustainable practices that ensure the longevity of herbal traditions.

- Remedies for common ailments, supported by modern research.

- How to create personalized healing plans using herbs and lifestyle changes.

This book is designed for beginners and seasoned herbalists alike, offering practical tips, detailed recipes, and evidence-based insights. It is a call to action for anyone who wishes to take control of their health in a natural and sustainable way.

Why Sustainability Matters in Herbal Medicine

Sustainability is not just a trend; it is a necessity. The global demand for herbal products has led to overharvesting, habitat destruction, and the exploitation of local communities. This section emphasizes the importance of sustainable practices in preserving nature's pharmacy for future generations.

Key takeaways include:

- The environmental impact of unsustainable herbal practices.

- How individuals can make a difference through ethical sourcing and cultivation.

- The role of education in promoting responsible herbalism.

By understanding the principles of sustainability, you'll be equipped to use herbal remedies in a way that respects both the environment and the people who depend on it.

Conclusion: A Journey into Nature's Pharmacy

The chapter concludes with an invitation to embark on a transformative journey into the world of herbal medicine. It sets the tone for the rest of the book, encouraging readers to approach natural healing with curiosity, responsibility, and an open heart.

Key closing thoughts:

- Healing is a journey, not a destination.

- Nature provides everything we need, but it's up to us to use it wisely.

- By combining ancient wisdom with modern science, we can create a sustainable future for herbal medicine.

Chapter 2: Nature's Pharmacy: Principles and Practices

The Basics of Herbal Medicine

Herbal medicine, also known as phytotherapy, is one of the oldest forms of healthcare. It involves the use of plants and their extracts to treat illnesses, promote healing, and maintain overall well-being. This chapter introduces the foundational principles of herbal medicine, helping readers understand how plants interact with the body to support health.

Key topics covered include:

- **What is Herbal Medicine?** A detailed explanation of how plants are used for medicinal purposes, from leaves and roots to flowers and seeds.

- **The Active Compounds in Herbs:** Understanding alkaloids, flavonoids, tannins, and other phytochemicals that give herbs their healing properties.

- **Whole Plant vs. Isolated Compounds:** Why the synergistic effect of using the whole plant often outperforms isolated chemical extracts.

By the end of this section, readers will appreciate that herbal medicine isn't just about treating symptoms—it's about restoring balance to the body and mind.

The Role of Nature in Healing

Plants are an integral part of Earth's ecosystems, playing a vital role in the health of all living organisms. This section delves into the profound relationship between humans and plants, exploring how this connection fosters healing.

Topics include:

- **The Evolutionary Bond Between Humans and Plants:**
  How our ancestors discovered the medicinal properties of plants and passed this knowledge down through generations.

- **The Energetics of Herbs:**
  A look at traditional systems like Ayurveda and Traditional Chinese Medicine, which classify herbs by their energetic qualities (e.g., warming, cooling, moistening, drying).

- **Healing Through Connection to Nature:**
  How spending time in natural environments, such as forests or gardens, enhances physical and mental well-being.

This section also introduces the idea that healing is not just about taking herbs but about reconnecting with the natural world in a holistic way.

Sustainability in Herbal Practices

With the growing popularity of herbal medicine, sustainability has become a critical issue. Overharvesting, habitat destruction, and unethical sourcing practices threaten the very plants we rely on for healing. This section teaches readers how to ensure their herbal practices are sustainable and respectful of nature.

Key points include:

- **The Environmental Impact of Overharvesting:** The consequences of unsustainable herb collection, including the endangerment of species like wild ginseng and goldenseal.

- **Sustainable Sourcing Tips:**

  o Support ethical suppliers who practice fair trade.

  o Choose certified organic herbs to avoid harmful pesticides.

  o Opt for locally grown or wildcrafted herbs where possible.

- **Conservation Efforts in Herbal Medicine:** Examples of initiatives aimed at preserving medicinal plants, such as botanical gardens and seed banks.

Readers will learn practical steps they can take to ensure that their use of herbal medicine supports the environment rather than harming it.

[18]

Building Your Own Nature's Pharmacy

One of the most empowering aspects of herbal medicine is the ability to create your own remedies using plants you grow or source sustainably. This section provides readers with the tools they need to start building their own "nature's pharmacy."

Topics include:

- **Choosing the Right Herbs for Your Needs:** A guide to selecting versatile, beginner-friendly herbs like chamomile, peppermint, and calendula.

- **Growing Herbs at Home:**

    o Tips for growing herbs in a garden, on a balcony, or even indoors.

    o The importance of soil quality, sunlight, and watering schedules.

- **Harvesting and Storing Herbs:** How to harvest herbs at their peak potency and store them properly to preserve their medicinal properties.

This section empowers readers to take the first steps toward self-sufficiency in herbal medicine.

The Ethical Use of Herbal Remedies

Herbs are powerful allies in healing, but they must be used responsibly. This section emphasizes the importance of ethical and safe practices in herbal medicine.

Key topics include:

- **Herbal Safety Guidelines:**

    o Understanding proper dosages.

    o Recognizing potential interactions with medications.

    o Being cautious with strong or toxic herbs.

- **Respecting Cultural Traditions:** Many herbs have deep cultural significance. This section discusses the importance of respecting Indigenous knowledge and practices when using traditional herbs.

- **Sharing Knowledge Responsibly:** Encouraging readers to share herbal knowledge in a way that promotes education and sustainability.

By adopting an ethical approach to herbal medicine, readers can ensure that their healing journey benefits not only themselves but also the wider community.

Conclusion: A Commitment to Sustainability and Healing

The chapter closes with a call to action, encouraging readers to embrace the principles of nature's pharmacy in their daily lives. It emphasizes that herbal medicine is more than a set of practices—it's a way of life that fosters harmony with nature.

Key closing thoughts:

- Herbal medicine offers a sustainable path to health and well-being.

- By practicing sustainability and ethics, we can preserve nature's pharmacy for future generations.

- Healing with herbs is a journey of connection—to plants, to the Earth, and to ourselves.

Chapter 3: The Science Behind Herbal Remedies

Introduction to the Science of Herbal Medicine

Herbal medicine bridges the gap between ancient wisdom and modern science. While traditional systems relied on observation and experience, today's science has provided a deeper understanding of how herbs work at a biochemical level. This chapter dives into the science behind herbal remedies, offering readers a foundational understanding of the mechanisms that make herbs effective.

Key topics include:

- The evolution of herbal knowledge from folklore to pharmacology.
- How scientific studies validate traditional herbal uses.
- The role of phytochemicals in healing.

Phytochemicals: The Healing Compounds in Plants

Phytochemicals are the active compounds in plants responsible for their therapeutic effects. Each herb contains a unique combination of these chemicals, which work together to promote healing.

Key phytochemical groups and their effects:

1. **Alkaloids:** Potent compounds with a wide range of effects, including pain relief (e.g., morphine from opium poppy) and muscle relaxation (e.g., berberine).

2. **Flavonoids:** Powerful antioxidants that reduce inflammation and support cardiovascular health (e.g., quercetin in onions and berries).

3. **Tannins:** Astringent compounds that help tighten tissues and reduce swelling (e.g., in witch hazel and oak bark).

4. **Saponins:** Compounds that boost immune function and lower cholesterol (e.g., in ginseng and licorice root).

5. **Essential Oils:** Volatile compounds with antimicrobial and mood-enhancing properties (e.g., in lavender and eucalyptus).

This section explains how these phytochemicals interact with the body to produce therapeutic effects and why whole-plant remedies are often more effective than isolated compounds.

How Herbs Work in the Body

Herbal remedies work by interacting with the body's systems to restore balance and support natural healing processes. This section covers:

- **Adaptogens:** Herbs like ashwagandha and rhodiola help the body adapt to stress by regulating hormones and improving resilience.

- **Anti-Inflammatory Action:** Herbs like turmeric and ginger reduce inflammation by inhibiting pro-inflammatory enzymes.

- **Antimicrobial Properties:** Herbs like garlic and oregano fight infections by targeting bacteria, viruses, and fungi.

- **Nervine Effects:** Herbs like chamomile and valerian calm the nervous system and promote relaxation.

Scientific evidence and case studies are included to illustrate how these mechanisms work in practice.

The Synergy of Herbal Compounds

One of the most fascinating aspects of herbal medicine is the concept of synergy—the idea that the combined effect of a plant's compounds is greater than the sum of its parts. Unlike synthetic drugs, which often isolate a single active ingredient, herbs work holistically.

Topics covered:

[24]

- **Whole-Plant Medicine:** Why the diverse array of compounds in a single herb often leads to better outcomes.

- **Herbal Combinations:** How blending herbs can enhance their individual effects (e.g., combining valerian and passionflower for sleep support).

- **The Entourage Effect:** A concept borrowed from cannabis research, illustrating how multiple compounds work together for therapeutic benefit.

This section helps readers understand why herbal remedies are uniquely effective compared to many synthetic medicines.

Traditional Wisdom Meets Modern Science

Herbal medicine has been used for millennia, but how do ancient practices align with modern research? This section explores the intersection of traditional wisdom and contemporary science.

Key points include:

- **Validation of Traditional Uses:** Examples of herbs whose traditional uses have been confirmed by modern studies (e.g., milk thistle for liver health, echinacea for immune support).

- **Integration of Herbal Medicine into Modern Healthcare:** How hospitals and clinics are increasingly incorporating herbal remedies into treatment plans.

- **Challenges in Research:** The complexity of studying herbs due to their multifaceted composition and interactions.

Anecdotes of specific herbs and their journey from folk medicine to clinical use make this section engaging and informative.

Safety and Efficacy in Herbal Medicine

While herbs are generally safe when used correctly, understanding their potential risks is crucial. This section covers:

- **Standardization in Herbal Products:** How standardized extracts ensure consistent dosing and quality.

- **Potential Side Effects:** Common side effects of popular herbs and how to minimize risks.

- **Interactions with Medications:** Examples of herbs that may interact with pharmaceutical drugs (e.g., St. John's Wort and antidepressants).

Readers are provided with guidelines to use herbs safely and effectively, emphasizing the importance of consulting a healthcare professional when in doubt.

The Future of Herbal Science

As interest in herbal medicine grows, so does the research into its potential. This section explores exciting developments in the field, such as:

- **Herbal Genomics:** Using genetic analysis to understand how herbs affect individuals differently.

- **Nanotechnology in Herbal Medicine:** Enhancing the delivery and bioavailability of herbal compounds.

- **New Discoveries:** Emerging herbs and their potential uses in medicine.

This forward-looking section inspires readers to view herbal medicine as a dynamic and evolving field.

Conclusion: Embracing the Science of Nature

The chapter concludes by emphasizing the importance of understanding the science behind herbal remedies. By combining traditional wisdom with modern research, we can unlock the full potential of nature's pharmacy.

Key takeaways:

- The healing power of herbs lies in their complex chemistry and synergy.

- Modern science is continually validating and expanding our understanding of herbal medicine.

- A scientific approach to herbs enhances their safe and effective use in everyday life.

Chapter 4: Top Healing Herbs and Their Benefits

Introduction to Nature's Healers

Herbs have been humanity's most trusted healers for centuries. Each herb is a powerhouse of nutrients, phytochemicals, and energy, uniquely suited to address a variety of health concerns. This chapter serves as a guide to some of the most versatile and effective healing herbs, focusing on their health benefits, traditional uses, and modern applications.

Key Herbs for Everyday Use

This section introduces 12 foundational herbs that are easy to use, widely available, and beneficial for a range of health issues. Each herb is detailed with its common uses, benefits, and tips for incorporating it into daily life.

1. **Turmeric (Curcuma longa)**

   o **Benefits:** Anti-inflammatory, antioxidant, supports joint health, improves digestion.

   o **Uses:** Golden milk, spice in cooking, or as a supplement.

   o **Scientific Backing:** Contains curcumin, a potent anti-inflammatory compound supported by extensive research for arthritis and chronic inflammation.

2. **Chamomile (Matricaria chamomilla)**

   o **Benefits:** Calms the nervous system, aids digestion, supports restful sleep.

   o **Uses:** Tea, compresses, or as a mild sedative.

   o **Tip:** Ideal for children with colic or upset stomachs.

3. **Ginger (Zingiber officinale)**

   o **Benefits:** Relieves nausea, soothes inflammation, improves circulation.

   o **Uses:** Fresh in tea, grated in meals, or as ginger syrup for colds.

   o **Scientific Insight:** Studies show its efficacy in reducing nausea from motion sickness and chemotherapy.

4. **Elderberry (Sambucus nigra)**

   o **Benefits:** Boosts immune function, reduces cold and flu duration, rich in antioxidants.

   o **Uses:** Syrup, lozenges, or infused in teas.

   o **Note:** Best taken at the onset of illness for maximum effect.

5. **Peppermint (Mentha piperita)**

- Benefits: Eases digestive discomfort, relieves headaches, clears sinus congestion.
- Uses: Tea, essential oil (for topical application), or fresh leaves.
- Tip: Inhaling peppermint oil can reduce tension headaches.

6. Garlic (Allium sativum)

- Benefits: Antimicrobial, lowers blood pressure, supports heart health.
- Uses: Fresh in meals, capsules, or as garlic-infused oil.
- Traditional Wisdom: Known as "nature's antibiotic" for its ability to fight infections.

7. Ashwagandha (Withania somnifera)

- Benefits: Adaptogen that reduces stress, improves energy, and enhances sleep quality.
- Uses: Powders mixed into milk, capsules, or tinctures.
- Scientific Backing: Studies confirm its role in reducing cortisol levels and improving overall resilience.

8. Calendula (Calendula officinalis)

- Benefits: Soothes skin irritations, reduces inflammation, promotes wound healing.

- o **Uses:** Salves, creams, or teas for internal and external use.
- o **Tip:** Excellent for sensitive skin and baby care.

9. **Milk Thistle (Silybum marianum)**

- o **Benefits:** Protects and detoxifies the liver, supports digestion.
- o **Uses:** Capsules, teas, or powdered seeds in smoothies.
- o **Key Compound:** Silymarin, known for its liver-protective properties.

10. **Echinacea (Echinacea purpurea)**

- o **Benefits:** Strengthens the immune system, reduces the severity of colds and flu.
- o **Uses:** Teas, tinctures, or capsules.
- o **Note:** Best used as a preventative or during the early stages of illness.

11. **Lavender (Lavandula angustifolia)**

- o **Benefits:** Promotes relaxation, alleviates anxiety, supports sleep.
- o **Uses:** Aromatherapy, teas, or infused oils.
- o **Tip:** Place dried lavender under your pillow for a restful night's sleep.

12. **Licorice Root (Glycyrrhiza glabra)**

- o **Benefits:** Soothes sore throats, aids digestion, supports adrenal health.

- o **Uses:** Teas, lozenges, or tinctures.

- o **Caution:** Prolonged use may raise blood pressure; use in moderation.

Seasonal and Regional Variations

Nature provides herbs that thrive in specific climates and seasons, making them ideal for addressing seasonal health needs. This section explores:

- **Spring Herbs:** Dandelion and nettle for detox and rejuvenation.

- **Summer Herbs:** Mint and basil for cooling and digestion.

- **Autumn Herbs:** Elderberry and astragalus for immune support.

- **Winter Herbs:** Cinnamon and ginger for warmth and circulation.

The section emphasizes the importance of using locally grown herbs to align with the seasons and reduce your carbon footprint.

Traditional Uses of Healing Herbs

Herbal medicine is steeped in cultural traditions, with each region of the world contributing its own unique practices. This section highlights traditional uses of key herbs:

- **Ayurveda:** Turmeric for inflammation, tulsi (holy basil) for respiratory health.

- **Traditional Chinese Medicine (TCM):** Ginseng for energy, reishi mushroom for longevity.

- **Native American Traditions:** Echinacea for immunity, yarrow for wound care.

- **European Herbalism:** Chamomile for relaxation, calendula for skin healing.

These examples illustrate the universal wisdom of herbal medicine across cultures and time.

Selecting Quality Herbs

Not all herbal products are created equal. This section provides practical advice for choosing high-quality herbs:

- Look for certified organic products to avoid pesticides.

- Choose reputable brands with transparent sourcing.

- When purchasing dried herbs, check for vibrant colors and strong aromas, which indicate freshness.

Incorporating Herbs into Your Daily Life

This section offers tips for seamlessly integrating herbs into daily routines:

- Start your day with a calming chamomile tea or energizing ginger tea.

- Add turmeric to your meals for its anti-inflammatory benefits.

- Use herbal-infused oils for skincare or massages.

Simple recipes like "immune-boosting elderberry syrup" or "soothing lavender pillow spray" are included for readers to try.

Conclusion: A World of Healing in Your Hands

This chapter concludes by encouraging readers to explore the diverse world of herbs and discover their personal favorites. Herbs are more than remedies—they are allies in health, connecting us to nature and its abundant healing power.

Key takeaways:

- Learning about a few versatile herbs can transform your health practices.

- Seasonal and regional herbs offer tailored solutions for specific needs.

- The journey into herbal healing is both empowering and sustainable.

Chapter 5: How to Prepare and Use Herbal Remedies

Introduction: Empowering Yourself with Herbal Knowledge

Preparing herbal remedies at home is a rewarding and empowering practice. It not only ensures the quality and purity of your treatments but also connects you deeply to the plants you use. This chapter provides step-by-step instructions for making a wide variety of herbal remedies, from teas and tinctures to salves and syrups. By the end of this chapter, readers will feel confident in creating their own herbal medicines tailored to their unique needs.

The Basics of Herbal Preparation

Before diving into specific remedies, it's essential to understand the foundational techniques of herbal preparation. This section covers:

- **Choosing the Right Form of Herbs:**
  - Fresh vs. dried herbs: When to use each.
  - Whole herbs vs. powders: How they affect potency and usage.
- **Measuring Herbs Properly:**

- Standard ratios for herbal teas, tinctures, and other preparations.
- Importance of using a kitchen scale for accuracy.

- **Essential Tools for Herbal Preparation:**
  - Glass jars, cheesecloth, double boilers, and strainers.
  - Why stainless steel and glass are better than plastic or aluminum for working with herbs.

This section sets the stage for success by emphasizing the importance of precision, cleanliness, and care.

Herbal Infusions and Decoctions

Herbal teas are one of the simplest and most effective ways to use herbs. This section explains the difference between infusions and decoctions and how to prepare each:

- **Herbal Infusions (for delicate plant parts):**
  - Best for leaves, flowers, and soft aerial parts (e.g., chamomile, mint, nettle).
  - **How to Prepare:**
    1. Boil water.
    2. Pour over herbs (1 teaspoon dried or 2 teaspoons fresh per cup of water).
    3. Cover and steep for 10–20 minutes.

[38]

4. Strain and enjoy.

- **Herbal Decoctions (for tough plant parts):**

  o Best for roots, bark, and seeds (e.g., ginger, cinnamon, licorice).

  o **How to Prepare:**

    1. Add herbs (1 tablespoon dried per cup of water) to a pot.

    2. Simmer gently for 20–30 minutes.

    3. Strain and drink.

This section includes tips for enhancing flavor and combining complementary herbs for targeted benefits.

Tinctures: Concentrated Herbal Extracts

Tinctures are alcohol-based extracts that provide a convenient and potent way to use herbs. This section details:

- **Ingredients Needed:**

  o Dried or fresh herbs, high-proof alcohol (e.g., vodka), and a glass jar.

- **How to Make a Tincture:**

1. Fill a jar halfway with dried herbs or three-quarters with fresh herbs.

2.   Cover completely with alcohol, ensuring no air pockets remain.

3.   Seal the jar and store it in a cool, dark place for 4–6 weeks, shaking it daily.

4.   Strain the liquid into a clean glass bottle and label it with the herb name and date.

- **Dosage Guidelines:**

    o   20–30 drops (1–2 mL) in water or tea, 2–3 times daily.

- **Non-Alcohol   Alternatives:** Instructions for glycerin-based tinctures for children or those avoiding alcohol.

Herbal Syrups: Healing and Tasty Remedies

Herbal syrups are ideal for soothing coughs and boosting immunity, especially for children or those who prefer sweeter remedies. This section includes:

- **How to Make a Basic Syrup:**

    1. Prepare a strong herbal decoction (e.g., elderberry, licorice root).

    2. Strain the liquid and simmer it down to half its volume.

    3. Add honey (1:1 ratio with the reduced decoction) and mix well.

4. Store in a sterilized bottle in the refrigerator for up to 3 months.

- **Popular Herbal Syrups:**
  - Elderberry syrup for colds and flu.
  - Ginger syrup for digestion and nausea.
  - Thyme syrup for respiratory support.

Recipes are provided for each.

Salves and Balms: Herbal Healing for the Skin

Topical remedies like salves and balms are excellent for cuts, burns, rashes, and muscle pain. This section explains:

- **Ingredients Needed:**
  - Herbal-infused oils, beeswax, and optional essential oils.
- **How to Make a Salve:**

1. Prepare an herbal oil infusion (e.g., calendula, comfrey).

   - Combine herbs with a carrier oil (olive, coconut) and heat gently for 2–4 hours in a double boiler.

2. Strain the oil and mix with melted beeswax (1 part beeswax to 4 parts oil).

3.   Pour into tins or jars and allow to cool before sealing.

- **Healing Salve Ideas:**
  - Calendula salve for dry or irritated skin.
  - Arnica salve for sore muscles and bruises.
  - Lavender balm for relaxation and minor burns.

Compresses and Poultices: External Herbal Applications

Herbal compresses and poultices are simple remedies for localized pain, inflammation, or infection.

- **Compress:**
  1. Soak a clean cloth in a strong herbal tea or decoction.
  2. Apply it to the affected area for 15–20 minutes.

Recommended herbs: chamomile for swelling, witch hazel for bruises, or rosemary for muscle pain.

- **Poultice:**
  1. Mash fresh herbs into a paste (e.g., plantain leaves for insect bites).
  2. Spread on the skin and cover with gauze or cloth.

These methods are particularly useful for wounds, sprains, or skin irritations.

Herbal Oils and Vinegars

Herbal oils and vinegars are versatile preparations for culinary, medicinal, or cosmetic use.

- **Infused Herbal Oils:**
    - Used for massage, skin care, or as a base for salves.
    - Example: St. John's wort oil for nerve pain.
- **Herbal Vinegars:**
    - Great for digestion and mineral absorption.
    - Example: Apple cider vinegar infused with dandelion or nettle for a mineral-rich tonic.

Step-by-step instructions are provided for both.

Safety and Storage of Herbal Remedies

Ensuring the safety and longevity of your herbal remedies is crucial. This section covers:

- **Storage Tips:**
    - Keep remedies in dark, airtight containers in a cool, dry place.

- Label each preparation with its name, date, and intended use.

- **Shelf Life of Remedies:**

  - Teas and decoctions: 24–48 hours (refrigerated).

  - Tinctures: 2–5 years.

  - Syrups: 2–3 months (refrigerated).

  - Salves: 6–12 months.

- **Signs of Spoilage:**

  - Mold, off-smells, or discoloration.

Conclusion: The Art of Herbal Preparation

Preparing herbal remedies is as much an art as it is a science. By mastering these techniques, readers can create personalized, effective remedies tailored to their needs. This chapter empowers readers to take charge of their health with confidence and creativity.

Key takeaways:

- Start with simple remedies like teas and syrups before progressing to tinctures and salves.

- Practice patience and precision in every step.

- Embrace the joy of crafting remedies that nurture both body and soul.

Chapter 6: Creating a Sustainable Herbal Garden at Home

Introduction: Growing Your Herbal Pharmacy

A home herbal garden is a step toward self-sufficiency and sustainability. By cultivating your own herbs, you can ensure their freshness, quality, and environmental impact. This chapter provides a comprehensive guide to starting and maintaining an herbal garden, whether you have a sprawling backyard, a small balcony, or even just a sunny windowsill.

Section 1: Planning Your Herbal Garden

Why Grow Your Own Herbs?

- **Freshness:** Harvest fresh herbs at their peak potency for better flavor and medicinal benefits.

- **Cost-Effectiveness:** Reduce the cost of buying dried herbs or herbal remedies.

- **Environmental Benefits:** Minimize packaging waste and carbon emissions associated with store-bought products.

- **Therapeutic Benefits:** Gardening itself is a stress-relieving and grounding activity.

Choosing the Right Location

- **Sunlight Requirements:** Most herbs need at least 6–8 hours of sunlight per day. Select a location that receives ample sunlight, whether it's a windowsill, patio, or garden plot.

- **Soil Quality:**
  - Herbs thrive in well-draining soil.
  - Enrich the soil with organic compost for added nutrients.

- **Space Considerations:**
  - Small spaces: Use pots, vertical gardens, or window boxes.
  - Larger spaces: Design a dedicated herb garden with separate sections for culinary, medicinal, and aromatic herbs.

Designing Your Garden Layout

- **Themed Gardens:**
  - **Culinary Garden:** Basil, parsley, thyme, oregano, chives.
  - **Medicinal Garden:** Chamomile, calendula, echinacea, valerian.

- Tea Garden: Peppermint, lemon balm, lavender, hibiscus.

- **Companion Planting:**

  - Pair herbs that benefit each other, like basil and tomatoes or mint and parsley.

  - Avoid planting invasive herbs like mint directly in the ground; use containers instead.

Section 2: Selecting the Right Herbs for Your Garden

Beginner-Friendly Herbs

Start with herbs that are hardy, easy to grow, and versatile:

- **Basil:** Great for cooking and stress relief.

- **Mint:** Excellent for teas and digestive health.

- **Thyme:** Antimicrobial and ideal for respiratory support.

- **Parsley:** A nutrient-packed garnish that aids digestion.

- **Calendula:** Beautiful flowers with skin-healing properties.

Region-Specific Herbs

Grow herbs suited to your local climate and soil:

- **Warm Climates:** Lemongrass, rosemary, oregano, sage.

- **Cool Climates:** Chamomile, chives, mint, yarrow.

- **Tropical Climates:** Turmeric, ginger, holy basil (tulsi).

Perennial vs. Annual Herbs

- **Perennials (grow back every year):** Thyme, mint, rosemary, oregano.

- **Annuals (need to be replanted yearly):** Basil, cilantro, dill.

Section 3: Planting and Caring for Your Herbs

Step-by-Step Planting Guide

1. **Prepare the Soil:** Loosen it to ensure proper drainage and mix in organic compost.

2. **Plant the Seeds or Seedlings:**

   o Follow the spacing recommendations on seed packets.

   o Plant at the right depth—too shallow, and they'll dry out; too deep, and they won't sprout.

3. **Watering:**

   - Herbs prefer consistent moisture but dislike soggy soil.

   - Water in the morning to avoid fungal growth.

Caring for Your Garden

- **Pruning:** Regularly trim herbs to encourage bushier growth and prevent them from flowering too early (bolting).

- **Fertilizing:** Use organic fertilizers or compost every 4–6 weeks.

- **Pest Control:**

   - Use natural methods like neem oil or companion planting (e.g., planting marigolds to deter pests).

   - Handpick pests like aphids or caterpillars if necessary.

- **Weeding:** Keep the area weed-free to prevent competition for nutrients.

Harvesting Tips

- Harvest in the morning when the oils in the leaves are most concentrated.

- Use sharp scissors or pruning shears to avoid damaging the plant.

- Avoid over-harvesting—leave at least two-thirds of the plant intact to allow regrowth.

Section 4: Sustainable Gardening Practices

Water Conservation

- Use drip irrigation or water herbs early in the morning to minimize evaporation.
- Collect rainwater in barrels for eco-friendly watering.

Organic Gardening

- Avoid synthetic fertilizers and pesticides.
- Use natural soil enhancers like compost, manure, or mulch.

Recycling and Composting

- Compost kitchen scraps, dead leaves, and garden waste to create a nutrient-rich soil additive.
- Repurpose old containers for planting to reduce waste.

Preserving Biodiversity

- Plant a variety of herbs to attract beneficial insects like bees and butterflies.
- Allow some herbs to flower and seed to support pollinators.

Section 5: Storing and Preserving Your Harvest

Drying Herbs

- Air-dry herbs by hanging them in small bunches in a cool, dark, and well-ventilated area.

- Use a dehydrator for quicker results while preserving potency.

Freezing Herbs

- Chop fresh herbs and freeze them in ice cube trays with water or olive oil.

- Ideal for herbs like basil, parsley, and dill.

Making Herbal Products

- Infuse oils or vinegars with fresh herbs for culinary or medicinal use.

- Create herbal sachets or potpourri with dried flowers and leaves.

Section 6: Indoor Herb Gardening

Growing Herbs Indoors

- Use pots with drainage holes and place them near a sunny window.

- Herbs like mint, basil, and chives thrive indoors.

Using Grow Lights

- LED grow lights are excellent for herbs that don't get enough natural sunlight.

- Set a timer to provide 12–16 hours of light daily.

Hydroponic Herb Gardens

- Explore compact hydroponic systems for growing herbs without soil.

- Benefits: Faster growth, less mess, and space efficiency.

Section 7: Building a Connection with Your Herbs

- **Mindful Gardening:** Treat gardening as a meditative and grounding practice.

- **Gratitude Practices:** Thank your plants as you harvest, acknowledging their contribution to your well-being.

- **Herb Journaling:** Keep a record of what you plant, how it grows, and its uses to deepen your understanding and connection.

Conclusion: A Sustainable Journey of Growth

Creating a sustainable herbal garden is more than just a practical activity; it's a way of nurturing your relationship with nature, your health, and the environment. Whether you're starting with a single pot of basil or designing a sprawling medicinal garden, every effort contributes to a more sustainable, self-reliant lifestyle.

Key takeaways:

- Growing your own herbs ensures quality, sustainability, and self-sufficiency.

- Even small spaces can support a thriving herbal garden with proper planning.

- Gardening is a journey of connection—with the earth the plants, and yourself.

Chapter 7: The Synergy of Herbs in Healing – Blending and Combining for Maximum Effectiveness

Introduction: The Power of Herbal Synergies

In the natural world, herbs rarely work in isolation. They interact, complement, and enhance each other's healing properties, creating a whole greater than the sum of their parts. This chapter delves into the art and science of blending herbs to amplify their therapeutic effects. Readers will learn how to craft effective herbal blends for teas, tinctures, salves, and more, as well as the foundational principles of creating balanced, targeted formulations.

Section 1: Understanding Herbal Synergy

What is Herbal Synergy?

- **Definition:** Herbal synergy occurs when the combined action of two or more herbs produces a stronger or broader effect than individual herbs used separately.

- **Examples of Synergy:**
  - Licorice root enhancing the effects of other herbs in a formula.

o Ginger boosting absorption of turmeric's curcumin for anti-inflammatory effects.

The Roles of Herbs in a Blend

When creating herbal formulations, each herb plays a specific role:

- **Primary (Active) Herb:** The main ingredient targeting a specific issue. Example: Chamomile for relaxation.

- **Supportive Herb:** Enhances the primary herb's action. Example: Lemon balm to complement chamomile for stress relief.

- **Catalyst (Harmonizer):** Helps balance or improve the overall formula's effectiveness. Example: Licorice root as a harmonizer in many blends.

- **Flavor or Buffer Herb:** Makes the remedy more palatable or reduces potential side effects. Example: Peppermint masking bitterness in teas.

Section 2: Principles of Herbal Blending

Key Factors to Consider

1. **Therapeutic Goal:**

   o Identify the purpose of the blend (e.g., digestive support, immune boost, stress relief).

- o Choose herbs that work synergistically to achieve that goal.

2. **Balancing Energetics:**
   - o Consider the herb's warming, cooling, drying, or moistening properties.
   - o Example: A blend for colds might include warming herbs (ginger, cinnamon) to counteract chills.

3. **Proportions in the Blend:**
   - o A typical ratio is 3 parts primary herb: 2 parts supportive herb: 1 part catalyst or flavor herb.
   - o Adjust proportions based on the strength of each herb and the desired potency of the blend.

4. **Safety and Compatibility:**
   - o Avoid combining herbs with conflicting actions (e.g., sedatives and stimulants).
   - o Be aware of potential contraindications or interactions with medications.

Section 3: Crafting Herbal Tea Blends

Herbal teas are a popular way to use synergistic blends. This section guides readers through creating their own customized blends.

Steps to Make a Tea Blend

1. **Choose Your Base Herb:**

   o Example: Peppermint for digestion or rooibos for a caffeine-free antioxidant base.

2. **Add Complementary Herbs:**

   o Example: Add fennel and ginger to peppermint for a digestive blend.

3. **Incorporate Flavor Herbs:**

   o Example: Add orange peel or cinnamon for a pleasant flavor.

4. **Mix and Store:**

   o Blend herbs thoroughly and store in an airtight container away from light and moisture.

Example Blends:

1. **Relaxation Tea:** Chamomile, lemon balm, lavender, and a pinch of peppermint.

2. **Immune Boost Tea:** Elderberry, echinacea, ginger, and rose hips.

3. **Digestive Tea:** Peppermint, fennel, ginger, and licorice root.

Section 4: Formulating Tinctures for Specific Needs

Tinctures allow you to combine the concentrated benefits of multiple herbs.

How to Create a Tincture Blend:

1. Select herbs with complementary actions.

2. Combine dried herbs in the desired ratio (e.g., 50% primary, 30% supportive, 20% catalyst).

3. Infuse in alcohol following the tincture-making process from Chapter 5.

Popular Tincture Blends:

- **Sleep Aid:** Valerian, passionflower, skullcap, and lemon balm.

- **Stress Relief:** Ashwagandha, holy basil, and licorice root.

- **Digestive Support:** Dandelion root, ginger, and fennel.

Section 5: Synergistic Topical Blends

Topical applications such as salves, oils, and compresses can also benefit from herbal synergy.

Blending for Salves and Balms:

1. Choose herbs with similar properties for a focused effect.

    o Example: Calendula and comfrey for wound healing.

2. Combine infused oils of the herbs.

    o Example: A pain relief salve with arnica and St. John's wort oil.

3. Add essential oils to enhance the blend.

    o Example: Lavender essential oil for relaxation or tea tree oil for antimicrobial effects.

Example Topical Formulas:

- **Muscle Soothing Salve:** Arnica, cayenne, and peppermint.

- **Skin Healing Balm:** Calendula, comfrey, and chamomile.

- **Anti-Inflammatory Compress:** Turmeric and ginger decoction applied to sore joints.

Section 6: Blending for Energetic and Emotional Support

Herbs can address not only physical ailments but also emotional and energetic imbalances.

Calming Blends:

- Use nervines like chamomile, lemon balm, and passionflower to soothe anxiety.

- Combine with adaptogens like ashwagandha for long-term stress resilience.

Uplifting Blends:

- Blend mood-boosting herbs like St. John's wort, rose petals, and holy basil.

Grounding Blends:

- Add warming, earthy herbs like ginger, cinnamon, and licorice root for stability and grounding.

Section 7: Common Herbal Combinations and Why They Work

Famous Herbal Duos and Their Synergy:

1. **Turmeric and Black Pepper:**

   o Piperine in black pepper enhances the bioavailability of curcumin in turmeric.

2. **Chamomile and Lavender:**

   o Both herbs are calming, but lavender adds a deeper relaxation element.

3. **Peppermint and Ginger:**

- Peppermint cools and soothes while ginger warms and stimulates digestion, creating a balanced digestive blend.

4. **Licorice Root and Echinacea:**

- Licorice root harmonizes and supports echinacea's immune-boosting effects.

Why These Combinations Work:

- Synergy arises from the complementary actions of the herbs, their ability to enhance absorption, or their ability to counterbalance side effects.

Section 8: Safety Considerations in Blending Herbs

- **Avoid Overloading Blends:** Too many herbs can dilute the effectiveness of a formula. Stick to 3–5 herbs per blend.

- **Check for Interactions:** Research each herb's interactions with medications or preexisting health conditions.

- **Test New Blends:** Start with small doses to ensure there are no adverse reactions.

Conclusion: The Art and Science of Blending Herbs

Crafting herbal blends is both an art and a science, requiring an understanding of each herb's properties and how they interact. By mastering this skill, readers can create remedies tailored to their unique needs, enhancing the healing power of nature's pharmacy.

Key takeaways:

- Herbal synergy amplifies the effectiveness of remedies.

- Blending requires knowledge of each herb's role, proportion, and safety.

- Practice and experimentation lead to confidence and creativity in crafting personalized formulations.

Chapter 8: Herbal Remedies for Common Ailments – Natural Solutions for Everyday Health Issues

Introduction: Embracing Nature's Pharmacy

Herbal remedies have been used for centuries to treat a wide variety of ailments, from minor aches and pains to chronic conditions. This chapter explores the healing properties of various herbs and provides practical guidance on how to use them for common health issues. By incorporating herbal remedies into your daily routine, you can tap into the power of nature to maintain and improve your well-being.

Section 1: Digestive Health – Soothing the Stomach and Gut

Herbs for Digestive Support

Digestive health is crucial for overall well-being, and herbs can play a significant role in improving digestion, alleviating discomfort, and promoting gut health.

1. **Peppermint (Mentha piperita)**
   - o **Benefits:** Relieves indigestion, bloating, and gas; soothes the stomach and intestines.

- **Use:** Drink peppermint tea after meals to aid digestion. A few drops of peppermint oil can be diluted in water or rubbed on the stomach to relieve discomfort.

2. **Ginger (Zingiber officinale)**

- **Benefits:** Stimulates digestion, reduces nausea, and alleviates bloating and gas.

- **Use:** Fresh ginger can be grated and steeped in hot water for tea or added to food. Ginger tincture can also help with nausea and motion sickness.

3. **Fennel (Foeniculum vulgare)**

- **Benefits:** Eases bloating, gas, and indigestion; promotes the secretion of digestive enzymes.

- **Use:** Drink fennel tea after meals or chew fennel seeds to relieve gas and bloating.

4. **Dandelion (Taraxacum officinale)**

- **Benefits:** Stimulates bile production, supports liver detoxification, and aids in digestion.

- **Use:** Drink dandelion root tea or use dandelion leaf in salads. Dandelion root tincture can also support liver health.

Section 2: Immune System Boost – Strengthening Your Body's Defenses

Herbal remedies can support the immune system, helping to prevent illness and boost the body's ability to fight infections.

1. **Echinacea (Echinacea purpurea)**

   o **Benefits:** Stimulates immune function, helps reduce the duration of colds and flu.

   o **Use:** Echinacea can be taken as a tincture, tea, or capsules. It is most effective when taken at the onset of cold symptoms.

2. **Elderberry (Sambucus nigra)**

   o **Benefits:** Rich in antioxidants, it helps fight viruses, particularly during the cold and flu season.

   o **Use:** Elderberry syrup is a popular remedy for colds and flu. It can also be used as a preventative measure.

3. **Astragalus (Astragalus membranaceus)**

   o **Benefits:** Enhances immune function and helps protect against viral and bacterial infections.

   o **Use:** Astragalus root can be taken as a tea, tincture, or in capsule form.

4. **Garlic (Allium sativum)**

- o **Benefits:** Known for its antimicrobial, antifungal, and immune-boosting properties.

- o **Use:** Fresh garlic can be eaten raw, added to food, or used in garlic oil. Garlic supplements or tinctures also provide therapeutic benefits.

Section 3: Stress and Anxiety – Calming the Mind and Body

Herbs can have a profound impact on emotional and mental health, helping to reduce stress, anxiety, and promote relaxation.

1. **Lavender (Lavandula angustifolia)**

   - o **Benefits:** Known for its calming and soothing effects; helps alleviate stress, anxiety, and insomnia.

   - o **Use:** Lavender essential oil can be diffused or applied topically with a carrier oil. Lavender tea is also effective for relaxation.

2. **Chamomile (Matricaria chamomilla)**

   - o **Benefits:** Promotes relaxation, reduces anxiety, and improves sleep quality.

   - o **Use:** Chamomile tea is ideal for evening relaxation. Chamomile tincture can also be taken for more immediate effects.

3. **Ashwagandha (Withania somnifera)**

   o **Benefits:** An adaptogen that helps the body cope with stress and enhances resilience.

   o **Use:** Ashwagandha is available in capsule, powder, and tincture forms. It can be taken daily to support long-term stress management.

4. **Lemon Balm (Melissa officinalis)**

   o **Benefits:** Helps calm the nervous system, reduce anxiety, and improve mood.

   o **Use:** Lemon balm tea is ideal for unwinding and calming the mind. It can also be added to bathwater for a relaxing soak.

Section 4: Skin Health – Healing and Nourishing the Skin

Herbs have been used for centuries to treat skin conditions, heal wounds, and nourish the skin.

1. **Calendula (Calendula officinalis)**

   o **Benefits:** Promotes wound healing, soothes irritated skin, and has anti-inflammatory properties.

   o **Use:** Calendula can be applied topically as a salve or infused oil for skin rashes, cuts, or burns. Calendula tea can also be used to wash inflamed skin.

2. **Aloe Vera (Aloe barbadensis)**

   o **Benefits:** Hydrates and soothes sunburns, minor burns, and skin irritation.

   o **Use:** Aloe vera gel can be applied directly to the skin for quick relief. It can also be consumed for internal healing.

3. **Tea Tree Oil (Melaleuca alternifolia)**

   o **Benefits:** Antibacterial and antifungal properties; helps treat acne, fungal infections, and minor wounds.

   o **Use:** Tea tree oil should be diluted with a carrier oil before applying to the skin. It can also be added to homemade skin-care products.

4. **Comfrey (Symphytum officinale)**

   o **Benefits:** Promotes tissue regeneration and reduces inflammation; ideal for treating bruises, sprains, and burns.

   o **Use:** Comfrey can be used topically in the form of poultices, salves, or infused oils. It is important to use comfrey externally only, as internal use can be toxic.

Section 5: Sleep and Relaxation – Finding Restful Sleep Naturally

Many herbs can promote restful sleep and help combat insomnia without the need for pharmaceutical sleep aids.

1. **Valerian (Valeriana officinalis)**

   - **Benefits:** Known for its sedative effects; helps improve sleep quality and reduce anxiety.

   - **Use:** Valerian root can be taken as a tincture, capsule, or tea about 30 minutes before bed.

2. **Passionflower (Passiflora incarnata)**

   - **Benefits:** Calms the nervous system and aids in falling asleep.

   - **Use:** Passionflower can be consumed as tea or in tincture form. It is especially helpful for those who experience anxiety-induced insomnia.

3. **Hops (Humulus lupulus)**

   - **Benefits:** Often used in combination with other herbs to treat insomnia and nervous tension.

   - **Use:** Hops can be taken as a tea or in tincture form. It is particularly useful when combined with valerian or passionflower.

4. **Skullcap (Scutellaria lateriflora)**

   - **Benefits:** Acts as a mild sedative, helping to relax the mind and promote restful sleep.

[70]

- o **Use:** Skullcap tea or tincture can be consumed before bedtime for a relaxing effect.

Section 6: Pain and Inflammation – Natural Relief for Discomfort

Herbs can provide relief from chronic pain and inflammation, reducing the need for pharmaceutical interventions.

1. **Turmeric (Curcuma longa)**

   - o **Benefits:** Contains curcumin, a potent anti-inflammatory compound that helps with pain and joint inflammation.

   - o **Use:** Turmeric can be consumed in food or as a supplement. It is most effective when combined with black pepper for improved absorption.

2. **Arnica (Arnica montana)**

   - o **Benefits:** Reduces pain, bruising, and swelling.

   - o **Use:** Arnica is typically applied topically in the form of a cream, ointment, or tincture. It is especially useful for treating muscle strains, sprains, and bruises.

3. **Willow Bark (Salix alba)**

- o **Benefits:** Contains salicin, which is similar to aspirin and helps reduce pain and inflammation.

- o **Use:** Willow bark can be taken as a tea or tincture for joint pain, headaches, and menstrual cramps.

4. **Ginger (Zingiber officinale)**

- o **Benefits:** Has natural anti-inflammatory properties and can help relieve pain, especially in the joints.

- o **Use:** Fresh ginger can be added to food, steeped in hot water for tea, or taken as a supplement.

Conclusion: Nature's Healing Touch

Herbs offer a safe, effective, and holistic approach to managing common health ailments. By incorporating these natural remedies into your routine, you can promote better health and well-being, free from the side effects often associated with pharmaceutical drugs. Whether you are seeking relief

Chapter 9: Herbal Remedies for Chronic Conditions – Supporting Long-Term Health and Wellness

Introduction: Addressing Long-Term Health with Herbs

Chronic health conditions, such as diabetes, heart disease, arthritis, and autoimmune disorders, require ongoing management and support. While herbs cannot replace medical treatments, they can complement conventional therapies by supporting the body's natural healing processes. This chapter explores how specific herbs can aid in the management of chronic conditions, reduce symptoms, and improve quality of life. The goal is to empower readers to take a proactive role in their health through the integration of herbal remedies into a comprehensive wellness plan.

Section 1: Diabetes Management – Regulating Blood Sugar Naturally

Diabetes is a condition characterized by elevated blood sugar levels. Many herbs have shown potential in supporting blood sugar regulation and improving insulin sensitivity.

1. **Cinnamon (Cinnamomum verum)**

   o **Benefits:** Helps improve insulin sensitivity and lower blood sugar levels.

   o **Use:** Sprinkle cinnamon on food or add it to tea. Cinnamon extract or capsules can also be taken for more concentrated effects.

2. **Fenugreek (Trigonella foenum-graecum)**

   o **Benefits:** Contains soluble fiber that helps regulate blood sugar levels and improve insulin function.

   o **Use:** Fenugreek seeds can be soaked overnight and consumed in the morning. It can also be taken in capsule form.

3. **Ginseng (Panax ginseng)**

   o **Benefits:** Improves insulin sensitivity, reduces blood sugar levels, and helps with fatigue.

   o **Use:** Ginseng is available as a tea, tincture, or in capsule form. It should be used with caution in people with certain conditions.

4. **Bitter Melon (Momordica charantia)**

   o **Benefits:** Contains compounds that mimic insulin, which helps lower blood sugar.

   o **Use:** Bitter melon can be consumed as a vegetable in meals, or taken in capsule form or as a juice.

Section 2: Heart Health – Strengthening the Cardiovascular System

Herbs can play a role in reducing the risk of heart disease by improving circulation, reducing cholesterol, and lowering blood pressure.

1. **Hawthorn (Crataegus spp.)**

   o **Benefits:** Improves circulation, strengthens heart muscles, and lowers blood pressure.

   o **Use:** Hawthorn extract or tincture can be taken daily to support heart health. Hawthorn tea can also be consumed.

2. **Garlic (Allium sativum)**

   o **Benefits:** Helps lower cholesterol levels, reduces blood pressure, and prevents plaque buildup in arteries.

   o **Use:** Fresh garlic can be consumed raw or added to food. Garlic supplements are also effective for cardiovascular health.

3. **Olive Leaf (Olea europaea)**

   o **Benefits:** Supports cardiovascular health, lowers blood pressure, and reduces cholesterol levels.

- o **Use:** Olive leaf extract is commonly taken in capsule or tincture form. Olive leaf tea is another option.

4. **Turmeric (Curcuma longa)**

- o **Benefits:** Contains curcumin, which has anti-inflammatory properties that support heart health.

- o **Use:** Turmeric can be consumed in food, tea, or as a supplement. It is best absorbed when taken with black pepper.

Section 3: Joint and Bone Health – Relieving Pain and Supporting Mobility

Chronic joint and bone pain, often due to conditions like arthritis, can be debilitating. Herbal remedies can help reduce inflammation, promote healing, and alleviate pain.

1. **Turmeric (Curcuma longa)**

- o **Benefits:** The anti-inflammatory properties of curcumin make turmeric effective for managing arthritis, rheumatoid arthritis, and general joint pain.

- o **Use:** Turmeric can be used in food, as a tea, or in supplements. Adding black pepper enhances the bioavailability of curcumin.

2. **Devil's Claw (Harpagophytum procumbens)**

   o **Benefits:** Known for its anti-inflammatory properties, it helps reduce pain and inflammation in the joints.

   o **Use:** Devil's claw is most effective when taken as a tincture or in capsule form for chronic joint pain.

3. **Ginger (Zingiber officinale)**

   o **Benefits:** Ginger has both anti-inflammatory and analgesic effects that can help alleviate joint pain.

   o **Use:** Fresh ginger can be added to food or tea. Ginger supplements are also available for more concentrated doses.

4. **Boswellia (Boswellia serrata)**

   o **Benefits:** An effective anti-inflammatory herb that helps reduce joint pain and stiffness, particularly in osteoarthritis.

   o **Use:** Boswellia extract can be taken as a capsule or tincture for long-term pain relief.

Section 4: Respiratory Health – Supporting the Lungs and Airways

Chronic respiratory conditions such as asthma, bronchitis, and COPD (chronic obstructive pulmonary disease) can benefit from herbal support to reduce inflammation, ease breathing, and strengthen lung function.

1. **Lobelia (Lobelia inflata)**

   o **Benefits:** Acts as an expectorant and bronchodilator, helping to clear mucus from the lungs and ease breathing.

   o **Use:** Lobelia is typically used in tincture form for acute respiratory issues. It should be used with caution and in low doses.

2. **Mullein (Verbascum thapsus)**

   o **Benefits:** Supports lung health by soothing the respiratory tract, easing coughing, and acting as an expectorant.

   o **Use:** Mullein can be used as a tea or tincture for lung support. It is gentle enough for long-term use.

3. **Eucalyptus (Eucalyptus globulus)**

   o **Benefits:** Helps clear mucus, reduces inflammation, and has a soothing effect on the airways.

- o **Use:** Eucalyptus oil can be inhaled through steam or used in diffusers. It can also be added to salves for chest rubs.

4. **Thyme (Thymus vulgaris)**

   - o **Benefits:** Known for its antimicrobial properties, thyme helps with respiratory infections, coughs, and congestion.

   - o **Use:** Thyme can be consumed as a tea or inhaled through steam. It can also be used in essential oil form for respiratory support.

Section 5: Autoimmune Conditions – Balancing the Immune System

Autoimmune diseases occur when the body's immune system mistakenly attacks its own tissues. Herbal remedies can help modulate the immune system and reduce inflammation.

1. **Ashwagandha (Withania somnifera)**

   - o **Benefits:** An adaptogen that helps regulate the immune system, reduce inflammation, and improve energy levels.

   - o **Use:** Ashwagandha can be taken as a tincture, capsule, or powder. It is best used over time for long-term support.

2. **Turmeric (Curcuma longa)**

- o **Benefits:** Curcumin in turmeric helps reduce inflammation, which is beneficial for autoimmune conditions such as rheumatoid arthritis and lupus.

- o **Use:** Turmeric can be added to food, tea, or taken as a supplement with black pepper for enhanced absorption.

3. **Nettle (Urtica dioica)**

- o **Benefits:** Nettle supports the immune system, helps reduce inflammation, and detoxifies the body.

- o **Use:** Nettle leaf can be consumed as a tea or in capsule form for long-term immune support.

4. **Astragalus (Astragalus membranaceus)**

- o **Benefits:** Modulates the immune system and has anti-inflammatory properties that are beneficial for autoimmune conditions.

- o **Use:** Astragalus is most effective when taken as a tincture or in capsule form.

Section 6: Mental Health – Enhancing Cognitive Function and Mood

Chronic mental health conditions, such as depression anxiety, and cognitive decline, can also benefit from herbal support. Certain herbs have been shown to improve brain function, boost mood, and reduce stress.

1. **Ginkgo Biloba (Ginkgo biloba)**

   o **Benefits:** Improves cognitive function, memory, and circulation, particularly in people with age-related cognitive decline.

   o **Use:** Ginkgo biloba is most effective when taken as a standardized extract in capsule or tincture form.

2. **Rhodiola (Rhodiola rosea)**

   o **Benefits:** An adaptogen that helps reduce stress, combat fatigue, and improve cognitive function.

   o **Use:** Rhodiola can be taken as a tincture, capsule, or powder for mental clarity and energy.

3. **St. John's Wort (Hypericum perforatum)**

   o **Benefits:** Known for its antidepressant effects, it helps regulate mood and alleviate symptoms of mild to moderate depression.

   o **Use:** St. John's Wort can be taken in tincture, tea, or capsule form, but it may interact with other medications, so caution is advised.

4. **Bacopa (Bacopa monnieri)**

o **Benefits:** Improves memory, cognition, and reduces anxiety. It is particularly helpful for those dealing with cognitive decline or high levels of stress.

o **Use:** Bacopa is typically taken as a capsule or powder for cognitive enhancement.

Conclusion: Empowering Long-Term Health with Herbs

Herbal remedies offer a natural and holistic approach to managing chronic health conditions. While they cannot replace conventional medical treatments, they can complement existing therapies by reducing symptoms, improving quality of life, and supporting overall health. By incorporating herbs into a well-rounded wellness plan, individuals can help manage chronic conditions with fewer side effects and enhance their long-term health. Always consult with a healthcare provider before starting any new herbal regimen, especially when managing chronic conditions or taking other medications.

Chapter 10: Herbal Remedies for Skin Health – Natural Solutions for Radiant Skin

---

Introduction: The Role of Herbs in Skin Health

Our skin is the body's largest organ and is constantly exposed to environmental stressors, aging, and various health conditions. Maintaining healthy skin is not just about aesthetics—it's a reflection of internal health. The skin can signal underlying issues such as hormonal imbalances, nutritional deficiencies, or immune dysfunction. Herbal remedies, rooted in tradition and supported by modern science, can be an effective and natural way to address skin concerns, reduce inflammation, and support the skin's healing process. In this chapter, we will explore the benefits of herbal treatments for common skin conditions, focusing on their ability to promote skin health, soothe irritation, and combat the signs of aging.

Section 1: Herbs for General Skin Health and Radiance

Healthy, glowing skin requires a combination of proper hydration, nutrients, and protection from the environment. Several herbs can provide vital antioxidants, vitamins, and minerals to support skin regeneration.

1. **Aloe Vera (Aloe barbadensis miller)**

   o **Benefits:** Aloe vera is renowned for its ability to hydrate and soothe the skin, particularly after sun exposure or minor burns. It also has anti-inflammatory properties that help reduce redness and irritation.

   o **Use:** Aloe vera gel can be applied directly to the skin, especially to dry or sunburned areas. Aloe vera juice can also be consumed for internal hydration, which reflects positively on the skin.

2. **Chamomile (Matricaria chamomilla)**

   o **Benefits:** Chamomile is known for its anti-inflammatory and calming properties. It is ideal for sensitive or irritated skin, reducing redness and providing a gentle healing effect.

   o **Use:** Chamomile can be used as a tea or in the form of an infused oil. It's also available as an extract for topical use in skin creams and lotions.

3. Lavender (Lavandula angustifolia)

- **Benefits:** Lavender has antiseptic, anti-inflammatory, and antioxidant properties. It helps to protect the skin from oxidative stress and aids in the healing of cuts, burns, and wounds. Lavender also has a calming effect, reducing stress, which can have a direct positive effect on the skin.

- **Use:** Lavender essential oil can be added to bath water or applied topically, diluted with a carrier oil. Lavender tea can also be consumed to promote relaxation, which benefits skin health indirectly.

4. Calendula (Calendula officinalis)

- **Benefits:** Calendula is known for its healing properties, making it a go-to herb for treating minor cuts, scrapes, rashes, and insect bites. It promotes tissue regeneration, speeds up wound healing, and helps soothe dry, irritated skin.

- **Use:** Calendula can be applied as a cream or oil directly to affected areas. Calendula tea can also be used as a gentle rinse for inflamed skin.

Section 2: Herbs for Acne – Combatting Breakouts and Managing Oily Skin

Acne is a common skin condition that affects people of all ages. It often results from hormonal fluctuations, stress, or bacterial overgrowth, leading to inflammation in the skin. Certain herbs can help control oil production, reduce inflammation, and balance hormones to keep acne at bay.

1. **Tea Tree Oil (Melaleuca alternifolia)**

   o **Benefits:** Tea tree oil is a potent antimicrobial and anti-inflammatory herb that helps reduce the bacteria that contribute to acne. It also soothes inflammation and controls excess oil production.

   o **Use:** Tea tree oil should be diluted with a carrier oil or cream before applying it to the skin. It can also be added to a face mask for deep pore cleansing.

2. **Neem (Azadirachta indica)**

   o **Benefits:** Neem has antibacterial, antifungal and anti-inflammatory properties, making it an excellent herb for treating acne. It helps reduce the spread of bacteria on the skin, calms inflammation, and promotes wound healing.

   o **Use:** Neem oil can be applied directly to acne affected areas. Neem leaves can be boiled to create a soothing tea, which can also be used as a face wash.

3. **Witch Hazel (Hamamelis virginiana)**

   - ○ **Benefits:** Witch hazel is a natural astringent that tightens the skin, reduces oil production, and helps soothe irritated skin. It's particularly beneficial for oily and acne-prone skin, as it helps reduce the appearance of pores and prevents breakouts.

   - ○ **Use:** Witch hazel extract can be applied directly to the skin with a cotton ball, or it can be used in homemade face toners to balance skin.

4. **Burdock Root (Arctium lappa)**

   - ○ **Benefits:** Burdock root is often used to purify the blood and support liver function, which can help alleviate acne caused by internal imbalances. It also has antibacterial and anti-inflammatory properties that can reduce breakouts.

   - ○ **Use:** Burdock root can be consumed as a tea or taken in capsule form. It can also be used topically in creams to reduce acne lesions.

Section 3: Herbs for Anti-Aging – Reducing Wrinkles and Supporting Skin Elasticity

As we age, our skin loses collagen, leading to wrinkles, fine lines, and a decrease in skin elasticity. Herbs can help stimulate collagen production, reduce oxidative stress, and promote cell regeneration, contributing to youthful, radiant skin.

1. **Rosehip (Rosa canina)**

   o **Benefits:** Rosehip oil is rich in vitamin C and essential fatty acids, which are crucial for collagen production and skin repair. It also has antioxidants that help combat oxidative stress, which accelerates skin aging.

   o **Use:** Rosehip oil can be applied directly to the face to reduce wrinkles and scars. It can also be used in face masks or added to creams for deeper hydration and regeneration.

2. **Gotu Kola (Centella Asiatica)**

   o **Benefits:** Gotu kola is known for its ability to stimulate collagen production and promote skin cell regeneration. It helps reduce the appearance of scars, stretch marks, and fine lines.

   o **Use:** Gotu kola can be consumed as a tea or taken as a supplement. It is also available in creams and ointments that can be applied to the skin.

3. **Ginseng (Panax ginseng)**

   o **Benefits:** Ginseng is an adaptogen that helps reduce the visible signs of aging by improving circulation, reducing wrinkles, and promoting skin elasticity. It also stimulates collagen synthesis, helping the skin appear firmer.

   o **Use:** Ginseng can be used in skincare products or consumed as a tea or supplement. It is commonly found in anti-aging creams and serums.

4. **Pomegranate (Punica granatum)**

   o **Benefits:** Pomegranate is a powerful antioxidant that protects the skin from free radical damage, which can accelerate the aging process. It also helps stimulate collagen production, keeping the skin firm and supple.

   o **Use:** Pomegranate extract can be found in many anti-aging serums and creams. Pomegranate seeds and juice can also be consumed for internal skin health.

Section 4: Herbs for Hyperpigmentation – Treating Dark Spots and Uneven Skin Tone

Hyperpigmentation, including age spots, melasma, and sun spots, occurs when excess melanin is produced in certain areas of the skin. Several herbs can help lighten dark spots, even skin tone, and reduce discoloration.

1. **Licorice Root (Glycyrrhiza glabra)**

   o **Benefits:** Licorice root has skin-brightening properties due to its active compound, glabridin, which inhibits the production of melanin and helps lighten dark spots.

   o **Use:** Licorice extract can be applied to the skin or used in a cream or serum. It can also be taken internally to help reduce pigmentation.

2. **Lemon Balm (Melissa officinalis)**

   o **Benefits:** Lemon balm has antioxidant properties and helps lighten hyperpigmentation. It also soothes skin irritation and provides a calming effect.

   o **Use:** Lemon balm can be applied as a topical extract or used in a facial steam to reduce dark spots.

3. **Turmeric (Curcuma longa)**

   o **Benefits:** Turmeric contains curcumin, which helps reduce the appearance of dark spots and uneven skin tone. It has both anti-inflammatory and skin-brightening properties.

- o **Use:** Turmeric can be applied as a face mask mixed with yogurt or honey. It can also be used in topical creams or serums.

4. **Papaya (Carica papaya)**

- o **Benefits:** Papaya contains enzymes, including papain, that help exfoliate the skin and lighten pigmentation. It also has antioxidant properties that protect the skin from further damage.

- o **Use:** Papaya pulp can be applied directly to the skin or used in face masks to lighten dark spots and improve skin texture.

Conclusion: Embracing Herbal Solutions for Skin Health

Herbs have a long history of use in skincare, providing natural, gentle solutions for a variety of skin concerns. From general skin health to acne, anti-aging, and hyperpigmentation, there is an herb for every skin issue. By integrating herbs into your skincare routine, you can harness the power of nature to support and enhance your skin's natural beauty. Whether used topically or internally, these herbs offer a holistic approach to maintaining healthy, glowing skin at every stage of life.

Chapter 11: Herbal Remedies for Mental and Emotional Well-Being – Supporting the Mind Naturally

Introduction: The Mind-Body Connection

Mental and emotional well-being are closely tied to physical health, and the effects of stress, anxiety, and depression can manifest in a variety of ways. The mind and body are intricately connected, meaning that when the mind is out of balance, the body suffers, and vice versa. Herbal remedies can offer a gentle and natural way to support mental and emotional health, helping to reduce stress, alleviate anxiety, improve mood, and promote cognitive function. This chapter explores herbs that have been traditionally used to support the mind, stabilize emotions, and enhance overall well-being, drawing on both historical and modern perspectives.

Section 1: Herbs for Stress Reduction – Calming the Nervous System

Stress is a natural part of life, but chronic stress can have detrimental effects on both the mind and body. The right herbs can help to reduce stress, calm the nervous system, and promote relaxation without causing drowsiness or dependence.

1. **Ashwagandha (Withania somnifera)**

   o **Benefits:** Ashwagandha is an adaptogen, meaning it helps the body adapt to stress and promotes a sense of calm and balance. It can lower cortisol levels (the stress hormone) and help reduce feelings of anxiety.

   o **Use:** Ashwagandha is commonly taken in capsule or powder form, but it can also be consumed as a tea or tincture. The root extract is particularly effective in promoting relaxation and reducing fatigue.

2. **Lemon Balm (Melissa officinalis)**

   o **Benefits:** Lemon balm is known for its calming effects and is often used to reduce anxiety and improve mood. It helps soothe the nervous system, making it useful for dealing with stress, nervous tension, and insomnia.

   o **Use:** Lemon balm can be consumed as a tea, or the fresh leaves can be applied topically to the skin to reduce tension. It is also available in tinctures and capsules for stress relief.

3. **Passionflower (Passiflora incarnata)**

   o **Benefits:** Passionflower is a gentle sedative herb that promotes relaxation and reduces anxiety. It has a mild calming effect that can help with both stress-induced insomnia and everyday anxiety.

o **Use:** Passionflower can be taken as a tea, tincture, or in capsule form. It is especially effective when combined with other calming herbs like valerian root for more profound relaxation.

4. **Lavender (Lavandula angustifolia)**

o **Benefits:** Lavender is one of the most well-known herbs for stress reduction and relaxation. Its aroma has been shown to reduce cortisol levels and promote a calm mind.

o **Use:** Lavender essential oil can be used in aromatherapy, added to a diffuser, or applied to the skin when diluted with a carrier oil. Lavender tea is also effective for promoting relaxation and sleep.

Section 2: Herbs for Anxiety and Depression – Natural Mood Enhancers

Anxiety and depression are common mental health challenges, and while they can be debilitating, certain herbs can provide relief by balancing neurotransmitters, stabilizing mood, and reducing emotional turmoil.

1. **St. John's Wort (Hypericum perforatum)**

o **Benefits:** St. John's Wort is perhaps the most widely studied herb for managing symptoms of mild to moderate depression. It is believed to work by increasing the availability of serotonin, dopamine, and norepinephrine, key neurotransmitters involved in mood regulation.

- o **Use:** St. John's Wort is most commonly taken as a supplement or in the form of a tea. It is important to consult with a healthcare provider before using this herb, as it can interact with certain medications, including antidepressants.

2. Rhodiola (Rhodiola rosea)

- o **Benefits:** Rhodiola is another adaptogen that helps the body cope with stress and fatigue. It has been shown to improve symptoms of anxiety and depression by increasing serotonin and dopamine levels in the brain.

- o **Use:** Rhodiola is typically taken in supplement form, although it is available as a tincture and powder as well. It is known for its ability to boost energy and focus while reducing feelings of anxiety.

3. Saffron (Crocus sativus)

- o **Benefits:** Saffron has been shown to have antidepressant effects, possibly due to its ability to modulate serotonin levels. It is especially effective for individuals suffering from mild to moderate depression and can help lift the mood.

- o **Use:** Saffron can be taken in supplement form, but it can also be added to food or drinks in small amounts for an uplifting effect. A few strands of saffron can be steeped in hot water to make a calming tea.

4. **Holy Basil (Ocimum sanctum)**

- o **Benefits:** Holy basil, also known as tulsi, is a revered adaptogen that helps balance cortisol levels and alleviate symptoms of anxiety and depression. It is known for its mood-stabilizing properties and can reduce feelings of emotional overwhelm.

- o **Use:** Holy basil is commonly consumed as a tea or tincture. It is also available in capsule form for those looking to benefit from its mood-enhancing effects.

Section 3: Herbs for Cognitive Function – Supporting Mental Clarity and Focus

Cognitive health plays a vital role in maintaining mental well-being. Herbs that support brain function, memory, and mental clarity can help protect the mind from age-related decline and enhance focus, concentration, and learning.

1. **Ginkgo Biloba (Ginkgo biloba)**

- **Benefits:** Ginkgo biloba is one of the most well-researched herbs for improving cognitive function. It helps enhance memory, mental clarity, and focus by increasing blood circulation to the brain and reducing oxidative stress.

- **Use:** Ginkgo biloba is available in capsules, tablets, and tinctures. It can be taken daily to improve cognitive function and reduce mental fatigue.

2. **Bacopa (Bacopa monnieri)**

- **Benefits:** Bacopa is an herb traditionally used in Ayurvedic medicine to improve memory, learning, and concentration. It has been shown to support brain health by enhancing the communication between nerve cells and reducing anxiety-related cognitive decline.

- **Use:** Bacopa can be taken as a supplement or in powder form, which can be mixed into smoothies or taken with warm water. Regular use has been shown to improve cognitive performance over time.

3. **Lion's Mane Mushroom (Hericium erinaceus)**

- **Benefits:** Lion's mane is a medicinal mushroom known for its neuroprotective properties. It stimulates the production of nerve growth factor (NGF), which promotes the growth and repair of nerve cells. Lion's mane has been shown to improve memory, focus, and overall cognitive function.

- o **Use:** Lion's mane is available in powder, capsule, and tincture form. It can be added to coffee, tea, or smoothies to improve mental clarity and reduce brain fog.

4. **Gotu Kola (Centella Asiatica)**

- o **Benefits:** Gotu kola is another herb known for enhancing mental clarity and cognitive function. It improves circulation to the brain, supports memory, and may reduce anxiety and depression.

- o **Use:** Gotu kola is commonly consumed as a tea or in supplement form. It can also be applied topically in oils or creams to improve skin health and overall vitality.

Section 4: Herbs for Sleep – Restoring Balance Through Restful Slumber

Quality sleep is essential for mental and emotional well being. Many people struggle with sleep disorders like insomnia, which can exacerbate stress and anxiety Certain herbs can support deep, restful sleep and restore the balance needed for emotional health.

1. **Valerian Root (Valeriana officinalis)**

- Benefits: Valerian root is a powerful herb known for its sedative properties. It helps reduce anxiety, calm the nervous system, and promote deep, restful sleep without causing grogginess the next morning.

- Use: Valerian root can be consumed as a tea, tincture, or in capsule form. It is most effective when taken 30 minutes before bedtime to induce relaxation.

2. **Chamomile (Matricaria chamomilla)**

- Benefits: Chamomile is a gentle herb known for its calming effects. It has mild sedative properties that help reduce anxiety and promote restful sleep.

- Use: Chamomile is commonly consumed as a tea before bedtime. The calming aroma of chamomile essential oil can also be diffused in the room for additional relaxation.

3. **California Poppy (Eschscholzia californica)**

- Benefits: California poppy is a gentle sedative herb that helps with insomnia and anxiety. It has a calming effect that promotes a peaceful night's sleep.

- Use: California poppy can be taken as a tea or tincture. It is often combined with other herbs, such as valerian or passionflower, to enhance its sedative effects.

[99]

Conclusion: Herbal Support for Mental and Emotional Health

Herbs offer a natural, holistic approach to supporting mental and emotional well-being. From reducing stress and anxiety to enhancing cognitive function and promoting restful sleep, these herbs provide a range of benefits that can help individuals achieve a balanced, peaceful state of mind. By integrating these herbs into daily routines, individuals can support their mental health in a sustainable and non-invasive way. Always consult with a healthcare provider before starting any new herbal regimen, especially for those with underlying health conditions or who are taking other medications.

Chapter 12: Herbal Remedies for Skin and Beauty – Healing from the Outside In

Introduction: The Connection Between Skin Health and Overall Wellness

The skin, being the largest organ in the body, plays a significant role in our overall health. It acts as a barrier against environmental toxins, pathogens, and physical damage. When our internal systems are out of balance, it often shows on our skin, manifesting as conditions like acne, eczema, dryness, and premature aging. Herbal remedies, which work both from the inside out and outside in, can help maintain the skin's health, reduce inflammation, promote healing, and rejuvenate the complexion.

This chapter explores some of the most effective herbs for supporting skin health, including those that can be applied topically, taken internally, or used in combination to enhance the skin's appearance and function.

Section 1: Herbs for Hydration and Moisture

– Keeping the Skin Soft and Supple

One of the most important aspects of skin health is maintaining adequate hydration. Dry skin can lead to irritation, cracking, and even premature aging. Many herbs possess moisturizing properties that can help keep the skin hydrated and soft.

1. **Aloe Vera (Aloe barbadensis miller)**

   o **Benefits:** Aloe vera is renowned for its cooling and soothing properties. It hydrates the skin, accelerates wound healing, and reduces inflammation. Aloe vera is excellent for treating sunburns, burns, rashes, and dry skin.

   o **Use:** Aloe vera gel can be applied directly to the skin for immediate relief. It is available in many topical products, but fresh aloe gel from the plant is often the most effective. It can also be taken internally in juice form to promote overall skin health.

2. **Cucumber (Cucumis sativus)**

   o **Benefits:** Cucumber has a high water content making it an excellent hydrator for the skin. I also has cooling and anti-inflammatory properties that can help reduce puffiness and calm irritated skin.

- o **Use:** Fresh cucumber slices can be applied to the face as a soothing mask or eye treatment. Cucumber juice can also be consumed for internal hydration benefits.

3. **Hibiscus (Hibiscus rosa-sinensis)**

   - o **Benefits:** Hibiscus is rich in antioxidants, vitamins, and organic acids that help hydrate the skin and promote elasticity. It also has natural alpha hydroxy acids (AHAs) that help gently exfoliate dead skin cells, leaving the skin soft and glowing.

   - o **Use:** Hibiscus can be consumed as a tea or used topically in masks or creams. The flower's juice or oil can be applied to the skin for a rejuvenating effect.

4. **Chamomile (Matricaria chamomilla)**

   - o **Benefits:** Chamomile is not only calming to the mind, but it is also an excellent moisturizer for the skin. It soothes inflammation, reduces redness, and helps hydrate dry skin.

   - o **Use:** Chamomile tea can be applied topically as a soothing compress, or chamomile oil can be used to hydrate and calm sensitive or irritated skin.

Section 2: Herbs for Acne and Skin Infections – Fighting Inflammation and Bacteria

Acne and other skin infections are often caused by an overproduction of oil, clogged pores, or bacterial imbalances. Several herbs possess antibacterial, antifungal, and anti-inflammatory properties that help clear the skin and prevent breakouts.

1. **Tea Tree Oil (Melaleuca alternifolia)**

   o **Benefits:** Tea tree oil is a powerful antiseptic and antibacterial herb, making it ideal for treating acne and other skin infections. It helps reduce inflammation, kill bacteria, and prevent further breakouts.

   o **Use:** Tea tree oil should be diluted with a carrier oil before applying it directly to the skin. It can also be added to face washes or creams to treat acne and blemishes.

2. **Witch Hazel (Hamamelis virginiana)**

   o **Benefits:** Witch hazel is known for its ability to tighten the skin and reduce swelling and redness. It has astringent and anti inflammatory properties that make it effective in treating acne, minor cuts, and irritations.

   o **Use:** Witch hazel can be applied directly to the skin as a toner or used in facial masks to reduce oiliness and control acne.

3. **Neem (Azadirachta indica)**

- o **Benefits:** Neem is a powerful herb with antibacterial, antifungal, and antiviral properties. It is effective in treating acne, eczema, and other skin infections. Neem helps balance skin oil production and clear up blemishes.

- o **Use:** Neem oil can be applied directly to the skin, diluted with a carrier oil, or used in lotions and soaps. Neem leaves can also be used in a paste for acne treatment.

4. **Calendula (Calendula officinalis)**

- o **Benefits:** Calendula is a natural antiseptic that promotes healing, reduces inflammation, and helps combat bacteria and fungi. It is especially helpful for treating acne scars, eczema, and rashes.

- o **Use:** Calendula can be applied topically as a cream or salve to soothe inflamed or infected skin. Calendula-infused oil or tea can also be used to treat minor wounds or burns.

Section 3: Herbs for Anti-Aging – Promoting Skin Elasticity and Reducing Wrinkles

As we age, the skin begins to lose elasticity, leading to wrinkles, sagging, and fine lines. Several herbs can help promote skin elasticity, boost collagen production, and reduce the appearance of wrinkles, resulting in a youthful and radiant complexion.

1. **Gotu Kola (Centella Asiatica)**

   - **Benefits:** Gotu kola is an herb known for promoting collagen production and improving skin elasticity. It helps reduce the appearance of fine lines and wrinkles by boosting the skin's ability to regenerate.

   - **Use:** Gotu kola can be consumed as a supplement or tea to improve skin elasticity from the inside. It is also available in topical creams and serums.

2. **Rosehip Oil (Rosa canina)**

   - **Benefits:** Rosehip oil is rich in vitamins A and C, which are crucial for collagen production. It helps reduce the appearance of fine lines, scars, and pigmentation by promoting skin regeneration.

   - **Use:** Rosehip oil can be applied directly to the skin as a moisturizer, or it can be added to creams and serums to help combat signs of aging. It is commonly used in facial oils for its anti-aging benefits.

3. **Ginseng (Panax ginseng)**

   - **Benefits:** Ginseng is known for its antioxidant properties, which help fight free radical damage and protect the skin from environmental stressors. It has been shown to improve circulation, which helps deliver more nutrients to the skin, promoting a healthy glow.

- o **Use:** Ginseng can be consumed in supplement form, or ginseng extracts can be added to skincare products to reduce the appearance of wrinkles and boost skin vitality.

4. **Turmeric (Curcuma longa)**

- o **Benefits:** Turmeric is a potent antioxidant and anti-inflammatory herb that helps reduce signs of aging. It promotes an even skin tone, reduces pigmentation, and protects against oxidative damage, all of which contribute to a youthful appearance.

- o **Use:** Turmeric can be applied to the skin in face masks or serums, or it can be consumed as a supplement or added to food for its internal benefits.

Section 4: Herbs for Skin Rejuvenation – Enhancing the Skin's Radiance

For glowing, radiant skin, some herbs help rejuvenate tired, dull, and lifeless skin by increasing circulation, improving nutrient delivery, and detoxifying the skin.

1. **Rose (Rosa spp.)**

- Benefits: Rose petals are full of antioxidants and essential fatty acids that promote skin hydration and boost its radiance. They also have anti-inflammatory properties that help reduce redness and calm irritated skin.

- Use: Rose water can be sprayed directly onto the skin or used as a facial toner. Rose oil can be applied topically to enhance skin glow and reduce signs of aging.

2. **Ginger (Zingiber officinale)**

- Benefits: Ginger improves circulation, which helps the skin glow by increasing the flow of oxygen and nutrients to the skin. It also has anti-inflammatory properties that help reduce puffiness and redness.

- Use: Fresh ginger can be applied as a paste or extract in skincare products. Drinking ginger tea or using ginger essential oil can also benefit the skin.

3. **Fennel (Foeniculum vulgare)**

- Benefits: Fennel is known for its detoxifying properties and its ability to promote healthy digestion. It helps eliminate toxins from the body, which can reflect on the skin' appearance, giving it a clearer and more radian look.

o **Use:** Fennel tea can be consumed to support detoxification, and fennel oil can be used in facial oils to rejuvenate the skin.

Conclusion: Achieving Radiant and Healthy Skin Naturally

Herbal remedies for skin and beauty offer a natural, holistic approach to skincare, supporting the skin's health from within and from the outside. By incorporating herbs into daily routines—whether in the form of teas, topical applications, or supplements—individuals can experience enhanced hydration, clearer skin, reduced signs of aging, and an overall radiant complexion. The use of herbs for skincare offers an eco-friendly and sustainable option for those seeking a more natural, chemical-free approach to beauty.

As always, it is essential to consult with a healthcare provider before beginning any new herbal regimen, especially for those with existing skin conditions or sensitivities.

Chapter 13: Herbal Remedies for Digestive Health – Nourishing the Gut with Nature's Healing Power

Introduction: The Vital Role of the Digestive System in Overall Health

The digestive system is not only responsible for breaking down the food we eat and absorbing nutrients, but it also plays a critical role in our overall health. A well-functioning digestive system is essential for maintaining energy levels, immune function, and mental clarity. Digestive issues, such as bloating, constipation, indigestion, and acid reflux, can lead to discomfort and even impact the body's ability to absorb vital nutrients.

Herbal remedies have been used for centuries to support digestion, ease gastrointestinal discomfort, and promote a healthy gut microbiome. In this chapter, we will explore the best herbs for nurturing digestive health, preventing common digestive ailments, and maintaining long-term gut wellness.

Section 1: Herbs for Digestive Support – Promoting Efficient Digestion

1. **Ginger (Zingiber officinale)**

- Benefits: Ginger is one of the most well-known herbs for digestive health. It stimulates the production of digestive enzymes, which helps the stomach process food more efficiently. It also reduces nausea, bloating, and indigestion, making it an excellent remedy for digestive discomfort.

- Use: Ginger can be consumed in fresh, dried, or powdered form. It is commonly brewed into tea, added to smoothies, or taken as a supplement. For digestive discomfort, ginger can also be chewed raw or taken in capsule form.

2. **Peppermint (Mentha × piperita)**

- Benefits: Peppermint is soothing for the digestive tract, providing relief from indigestion, bloating, and gas. Its active compound, menthol, helps relax the muscles of the gastrointestinal tract, allowing for smoother digestion and reduced cramping.

- Use: Peppermint tea is a popular remedy for indigestion, but peppermint oil capsules can also be taken for relief from bloating and abdominal pain. For external application, peppermint oil can be diluted with a carrier oil and massaged into the abdomen to alleviate discomfort.

3. **Fennel (Foeniculum vulgare)**

- o **Benefits:** Fennel seeds are known for their ability to relieve bloating, gas, and indigestion. They contain compounds that help relax the muscles of the digestive tract and promote the release of gas, reducing discomfort. Fennel also has antimicrobial properties that support gut health.

- o **Use:** Fennel seeds can be chewed after meals or brewed into tea. Fennel tea is often used to alleviate bloating and improve digestion. Fennel supplements are also available for those who want a concentrated dose.

4. **Slippery Elm (Ulmus rubra)**

- o **Benefits:** Slippery elm is a soothing herb that forms a gel-like substance when mixed with water, which helps to coat and protect the digestive tract. It can relieve symptoms of acid reflux, heartburn, and irritable bowel syndrome (IBS).

- o **Use:** Slippery elm is typically consumed as a powder mixed with water or in capsules. The powder can be made into a soothing tea or taken with warm water to calm an irritated stomach.

Section 2: Herbs for Gut Health – Supporting the Gut Microbiome

1. ## Chamomile (Matricaria chamomilla)

   o **Benefits:** Chamomile is known for its calming and anti-inflammatory properties. It can help reduce gastrointestinal inflammation, relieve cramps, and ease indigestion. Chamomile also supports the healing of the gut lining and encourages the growth of healthy gut bacteria.

   o **Use:** Chamomile tea is widely used to support digestion and promote a relaxed gut. It can also be taken in tincture form or as a supplement to calm digestive issues.

2. ## Turmeric (Curcuma longa)

   o **Benefits:** Turmeric contains the active compound curcumin, which has potent anti-inflammatory and antioxidant properties. It supports digestion by improving bile production and promoting the healthy flow of digestive juices. It can also help heal leaky gut syndrome and reduce inflammation in the intestines.

   o **Use:** Turmeric can be consumed in food, as a tea, or in supplement form. For enhanced absorption, turmeric is often combined with black pepper, which enhances curcumin's bioavailability.

3. **Dandelion (Taraxacum officinale)**

   o **Benefits:** Dandelion root supports liver function and promotes the production of bile, which aids digestion, especially the breakdown of fats. It also helps detoxify the digestive system and encourages the growth of beneficial gut bacteria.

   o **Use:** Dandelion root can be consumed as a tea or in capsule form. The fresh leaves can also be added to salads for an extra digestive boost.

4. **Licorice Root (Glycyrrhiza glabra)**

   o **Benefits:** Licorice root is a powerful herb for soothing the digestive tract. It can help hea ulcers, reduce inflammation, and protect the stomach lining. It is also helpful for those suffering from acid reflux or heartburn.

   o **Use:** Licorice root is available in tea, extract, o capsule form. It should be used in moderation due to potential side effects such as high blood pressure with prolonged use.

Section 3: Herbs for Managing Common Digestive Ailments

1. **Constipation: Senna (Senna alexandrina)**

   o **Benefits:** Senna is a natural laxative that stimulates bowel movements by increasing muscle contractions in the intestines. It is effective for short-term relief of constipation and works by promoting regularity.

   o **Use:** Senna is commonly used in tea form or as a supplement. However, it should not be used for extended periods as it can cause dependence or discomfort.

2. **Indigestion: Caraway (Carum carvi)**

   o **Benefits:** Caraway is known for its ability to relieve indigestion and bloating. It soothes the stomach, relieves gas, and helps with indigestion caused by overeating or rich foods.

   o **Use:** Caraway seeds can be chewed after meals or brewed into a tea. They are also available in capsule or extract form.

3. **Acid Reflux: Marshmallow Root (Althaea officinalis)**

   o **Benefits:** Marshmallow root forms a mucilaginous substance that coats the digestive tract, helping to soothe irritation caused by acid reflux. It also helps to reduce inflammation and

[115]

support the healing of damaged tissues in the stomach lining.

- Use: Marshmallow root can be taken as a tea, tincture, or in capsule form to reduce acid reflux symptoms.

4. **Diarrhea: Blackberry Leaf (Rubus fruticosus)**

- **Benefits:** Blackberry leaves have astringent properties that can help treat diarrhea by tightening the tissues of the intestinal lining and reducing the loss of fluids.

- **Use:** Blackberry leaf can be made into a tea and drunk to help manage diarrhea. The leaves can also be used in extracts or powders for more concentrated benefits.

Section 4: Detoxification and Healing – Herbs for Cleanse and Repair

1. **Coriander (Coriandrum sativum)**

- **Benefits:** Coriander supports digestion and helps detoxify the gut by promoting the elimination of toxins. It also assists in the removal of heavy metals from the body and aids in the digestion of fats.

- **Use:** Fresh coriander can be added to salads, soups, or smoothies. Coriander seeds can be brewed into tea or taken as a supplement for detoxification.

2. **Cayenne Pepper (Capsicum annuum)**

   o **Benefits:** Cayenne pepper helps stimulate digestion by increasing circulation to the digestive system and promoting the production of digestive enzymes. It can also assist in detoxification by promoting sweating and cleansing.

   o **Use:** Cayenne pepper can be added to food, taken as a supplement, or used in a detox drink to help promote digestive health.

3. **Cleansing Tea Blends**

   o **Benefits:** A variety of herbs can be combined to create a detoxifying tea blend that helps cleanse the digestive system. Popular herbs include ginger, peppermint, dandelion, fennel, and nettle. These herbs support liver function, aid in digestion, and promote detoxification.

   o **Use:** These herbal blends are commonly available as pre-made teas or can be made at home by combining fresh or dried herbs. They should be consumed regularly to support digestive health and detoxification.

Conclusion: Empowering Digestive Health
Naturally

The digestive system plays a vital role in the body's overall wellness, and nourishing it with herbal remedies is an effective way to promote long-term health. By using herbs to support digestion, enhance gut health, and manage common digestive issues, we can achieve a balanced and thriving digestive system. However, it is essential to consult a healthcare provider before starting any new herbal regimen, especially for those with chronic digestive conditions or who are on other medications.

Nature offers an abundance of herbs that can support digestive wellness, help alleviate discomfort, and encourage the body to function optimally. By incorporating these herbs into your daily routine, you can cultivate a healthy gut and enjoy better overall health.

Chapter 14: Herbal Remedies for Stress, Anxiety, and Mental Clarity – Balancing the Mind and Body with Nature's Aid

Introduction: The Mind-Body Connection and the Importance of Mental Health

In today's fast-paced world, stress and anxiety have become common challenges for many people. Chronic stress can not only negatively affect mental well-being but can also take a toll on the body, contributing to conditions like high blood pressure, digestive problems, weakened immunity, and even chronic pain. The mind and body are deeply interconnected, and maintaining mental health is just as important as physical health.

Herbal remedies have been used for centuries to help manage stress, anxiety, and promote mental clarity. Many herbs act as adaptogens, helping the body cope with stress and restore balance, while others offer calming or mood-enhancing effects. In this chapter, we will explore the most effective herbs for relieving stress, calming anxiety, improving mental clarity, and supporting overall emotional well-being.

Section 1: Herbs for Stress Relief – Restoring Balance to the Nervous System

1. **Ashwagandha (Withania somnifera)**

   o **Benefits:** Ashwagandha is one of the most well-known adaptogenic herbs, known for its ability to help the body adapt to stress. It helps lower cortisol levels, the body's primary stress hormone, and promotes a sense of calm and relaxation. It also supports the adrenal glands, which play a key role in stress response.

   o **Use:** Ashwagandha can be taken in capsule or powder form. It is often added to smoothies or herbal teas. For best results, it is commonly used over time, as it helps build resilience against stress.

2. **Holy Basil (Ocimum sanctum)**

   o **Benefits:** Holy basil, or tulsi, is another powerful adaptogen that supports the body's ability to cope with stress. It reduces anxiety and promotes emotional balance by regulating cortisol levels. Holy basil also enhances mental clarity and supports healthy immune function.

   o **Use:** Holy basil can be consumed as tea or in capsule form. Fresh tulsi leaves can be added to meals or made into a refreshing herbal drink.

3. **Rhodiola (Rhodiola rosea)**

- o **Benefits:** Rhodiola is an adaptogen that enhances the body's resistance to stress while improving energy levels, mood, and mental clarity. It has been shown to reduce symptoms of anxiety and depression and improve cognitive function.

- o **Use:** Rhodiola is commonly available in capsules or tinctures. It can be taken in the morning or early afternoon to help improve energy and focus while reducing stress.

4. **Lemon Balm (Melissa officinalis)**

- o **Benefits:** Lemon balm is known for its calming effects on the nervous system. It can help alleviate anxiety, improve sleep, and ease stress. The herb has mild sedative properties, making it ideal for those who need help relaxing after a long day.

- o **Use:** Lemon balm is often consumed as a tea, but it is also available in tinctures and capsules. Fresh leaves can be added to water or used in cooking.

Section 2: Herbs for Anxiety – Calming the Nervous System

1. **Lavender (Lavandula angustifolia)**

- Benefits: Lavender is perhaps one of the most popular herbs for reducing anxiety and promoting relaxation. Its soothing fragrance helps calm the nervous system and can reduce symptoms of anxiety and insomnia. Lavender also has mild sedative properties, helping to ease restlessness.

- Use: Lavender can be used in essential oil form for aromatherapy. A few drops of lavender oil in a diffuser or applied to the wrists can provide calming effects. Lavender tea is also an excellent way to promote relaxation.

2. **Valerian Root (Valeriana officinalis)**

- Benefits: Valerian root is known for its ability to promote relaxation and sleep. It has a calming effect on the nervous system, making it helpful for individuals with anxiety-related insomnia. Valerian root also helps reduce the physical symptoms of anxiety, such as a racing heart and muscle tension.

- Use: Valerian root is available in capsules, tinctures, or as a tea. It should be used cautiously, as it may cause drowsiness. For best results, it is typically taken in the evening before bedtime.

3. **Passionflower (Passiflora incarnata)**

- Benefits: Passionflower is a calming herb that reduces anxiety by increasing the production of gamma-aminobutyric acid (GABA) in the brain. GABA is a neurotransmitter that helps to reduce nerve activity, creating a sense of calm and relaxation.

- o **Use:** Passionflower can be consumed as tea, tincture, or in capsule form. It is often used for anxiety, nervousness, and sleeplessness.

4. **Chamomile (Matricaria chamomilla)**

- o **Benefits:** Chamomile is a gentle yet effective herb for calming the nervous system. It has mild sedative effects, reducing anxiety, promoting sleep, and calming an overactive mind. Chamomile is particularly useful for stress-related digestive upset and mild insomnia.

- o **Use:** Chamomile is best consumed as tea, but it is also available in tincture and capsule form. A cup of chamomile tea before bed can help soothe the mind and prepare for restful sleep.

Section 3: Herbs for Mental Clarity – Enhancing Cognitive Function and Focus

1. **Ginkgo Biloba (Ginkgo biloba)**

- o **Benefits:** Ginkgo biloba is one of the oldest known herbal remedies for improving cognitive function. It enhances blood circulation to the brain, which can help improve memory, focus, and mental clarity. Ginkgo is also known to reduce symptoms of anxiety and stress by promoting relaxation.

- o **Use:** Ginkgo biloba is available in capsule, tablet, or liquid extract form. It is typically taken daily to support long-term cognitive health.

2. Gotu Kola (Centella Asiatica)

- o **Benefits:** Gotu kola has been used for centuries to support mental clarity, improve memory, and reduce stress. It is believed to stimulate the production of collagen and improve circulation to the brain, promoting cognitive function and mental clarity.

- o **Use:** Gotu kola can be consumed in capsule form or as a tea. It can also be found in topical creams for skin health, as it also promotes healing and regeneration.

3. Bacopa (Bacopa monnieri)

- o **Benefits:** Bacopa is an herb that has been used in Ayurvedic medicine to enhance memory, focus, and concentration. It is an adaptogen, helping to manage stress while improving mental clarity and cognitive function. Bacopa has been shown to improve mental performance, especially in stressful situations.

- Use: Bacopa is commonly available in capsule or powder form. It can be taken daily to improve memory, learning, and mental focus.

4. **Peppermint (Mentha × piperita)**

- **Benefits:** Peppermint is a stimulating herb that can help improve mental clarity and focus. It enhances cognitive function by increasing blood flow to the brain and stimulating the nervous system. Peppermint is particularly effective for combating mental fatigue and enhancing alertness.

- **Use:** Peppermint tea is a great way to boost mental clarity. Peppermint oil can also be used in aromatherapy to promote focus and relieve mental fatigue.

Section 4: Herbs for Mood Enhancement – Lifting Spirits Naturally

1. **St. John's Wort (Hypericum perforatum)**

- **Benefits:** St. John's Wort is widely used for improving mood and alleviating symptoms of mild to moderate depression. It works by increasing levels of serotonin, dopamine, and norepinephrine in the brain, which helps regulate mood and alleviate feelings of sadness or low energy.

- Use: St. John's Wort is most commonly consumed in capsule or tincture form. It is important to consult with a healthcare provider before using it, as it can interact with certain medications.

2. **Saffron (Crocus sativus)**

   - **Benefits:** Saffron has been shown to have mood-enhancing properties, helping to improve symptoms of depression and anxiety. It increases serotonin levels in the brain, helping to elevate mood and alleviate stress. Saffron is also known for its ability to boost energy and promote a sense of well-being.

   - **Use:** Saffron can be added to food and beverages, or taken in supplement form. It can also be consumed as an herbal tea.

3. **Lemon Balm (Melissa officinalis)**

   - **Benefits:** Lemon balm helps improve mood by reducing anxiety and promoting relaxation. It has mild sedative effects and can help elevate mood, particularly during times of stress or restlessness.

   - **Use:** Lemon balm tea is an excellent option for calming anxiety and lifting the mood. It is also available in tincture and capsule forms for more concentrated effects.

4. **Ginseng (Panax ginseng)**

- o **Benefits:** Ginseng is a powerful adaptogen that boosts energy, improves mental clarity, and supports emotional well-being. It helps reduce fatigue, improve concentration, and elevate mood, making it a useful herb for managing stress and lifting spirits.

- o **Use:** Ginseng can be consumed in tea, capsules, or powder form. It is often taken in the morning for a boost of energy and mental clarity throughout the day.

Conclusion: Cultivating Mental Wellness with Herbal Remedies

Herbal remedies offer a natural and effective way to support mental health and manage stress and anxiety. Adaptogens like ashwagandha and rhodiola help the body cope with the physical and emotional effects of stress, while herbs like lavender, lemon balm, and passionflower offer calming effects to soothe anxiety. Herbs such as ginkgo biloba and bacopa enhance cognitive function, providing clarity and focus for better mental performance.

By incorporating these herbs into daily life, we can create a balanced, calm, and clear state of mind. Always consult a healthcare provider before using herbs, especially if you are pregnant, nursing, or on medication, to ensure safety and effectiveness. With the right herbal support, you can nurture your mental health and enjoy a more peaceful, focused, and balanced life.

Chapter 15: Herbal Remedies for Digestive Health – Supporting a Happy Gut with Nature's Healing Power

Introduction: The Role of Gut Health in Overall Wellness

The digestive system is often referred to as the "second brain," and for good reason. It plays a crucial role in nutrient absorption, immune function, and overall health. A well-functioning digestive system supports energy levels, mental clarity, and emotional well-being. When digestive issues arise—such as bloating, constipation, acid reflux, or indigestion—it can have a significant impact on daily life and overall health.

Herbal remedies offer an effective and natural way to support digestive health. Many herbs have soothing, anti-inflammatory, and healing properties that help alleviate digestive discomforts, improve gut function, and promote better digestion. In this chapter, we will explore some of the most effective herbs for digestive health, as well as how they work to promote gut wellness.

Section 1: Herbs for Relieving Indigestion and Upset Stomach

1. **Ginger (Zingiber officinale)**

   o **Benefits:** Ginger is one of the most popular herbs for digestive support. It has been used for centuries to ease nausea, indigestion, and bloating. Ginger helps stimulate the production of digestive enzymes, which can improve digestion and reduce discomfort after meals. It also helps relax the muscles in the digestive tract, reducing gas and bloating.

   o **Use:** Ginger can be consumed fresh, as a tea, or in capsule form. For best results, consume ginger tea after meals to relieve indigestion or nausea. Fresh ginger can be grated into hot water or smoothies for added digestive benefits.

2. **Peppermint (Mentha × piperita)**

   o **Benefits:** Peppermint is another well-known herb that aids digestion. Its menthol content has a soothing effect on the muscles of the digestive tract, helping to relieve bloating, cramps, and indigestion. Peppermint also helps improve bile flow, which assists in the digestion of fats.

   o **Use:** Peppermint can be consumed as tea, or in the form of enteric-coated capsules, which help the herb reach the intestines. Peppermint oil can also be used in aromatherapy to alleviate nausea and digestive discomfort.

3. **Fennel (Foeniculum vulgare)**

   o **Benefits:** Fennel seeds have been used traditionally to relieve bloating, gas, and indigestion. The herb has antispasmodic properties, helping to relax the muscles of the intestines and reduce cramps. Fennel is also known to stimulate the production of bile, aiding in digestion and helping to prevent constipation.

   o **Use:** Fennel seeds can be chewed after meals to help with bloating, or you can brew fennel tea for a soothing digestive aid. Fennel supplements are also available for those who prefer a more concentrated form.

4. **Chamomile (Matricaria chamomilla)**

   o **Benefits:** Chamomile is well-known for its calming effects on both the mind and the digestive system. It soothes the stomach lining, reduces inflammation, and helps alleviate indigestion, gas, and bloating. Chamomile also promotes relaxation, making it an excellent herb for those whose digestive issues are triggered by stress.

   o **Use:** Chamomile is most commonly consumed as tea, but it can also be taken in capsule or tincture form. A warm cup of chamomile tea before bed can help promote restful sleep while soothing the digestive system.

Section 2: Herbs for Relieving Constipation and Promoting Regular Bowel Movements

1. **Senna (Senna alexandrina)**

   o **Benefits:** Senna is a well-known herbal remedy for constipation. It works as a natural stimulant laxative, increasing peristalsis (muscle contractions in the intestines) to help move stool through the digestive tract. It is particularly helpful for short-term constipation relief.

   o **Use:** Senna is available in tea or tablet form. It is typically used for occasional constipation, but should not be relied upon for long-term use, as it may lead to dependency.

2. **Psyllium Husk (Plantago ovata)**

   o **Benefits:** Psyllium is a fiber-rich herb that helps regulate bowel movements by absorbing water and adding bulk to stool. It is effective for both constipation and diarrhea. Psyllium husk is also beneficial for improving overall gut health by promoting the growth of beneficial bacteria in the intestines.

[132]

- o **Use:** Psyllium husk is often taken in powder or capsule form. It should be mixed with water or another liquid before consumption, as it expands when it absorbs liquid. It is important to drink plenty of water when using psyllium to avoid bloating or discomfort.

3. **Cascara Sagrada (Rhamnus purshiana)**

- o **Benefits:** Cascara sagrada is a natural stimulant laxative that works by stimulating the muscles of the colon to promote bowel movements. It has been used for centuries to treat constipation and is effective for relieving occasional digestive sluggishness.

- o **Use:** Cascara sagrada is available in capsule or liquid extract form. Like senna, it should only be used for short-term constipation relief to avoid dependency on the herb.

4. **Aloe Vera (Aloe barbadensis)**

- o **Benefits:** Aloe vera is well-known for its ability to soothe inflammation and promote healing. It also acts as a natural laxative, helping to relieve constipation by promoting bowel movements and soothing the digestive system.

- o **Use:** Aloe vera juice or gel can be consumed for digestive health, but it should be used with caution. Overuse can lead to diarrhea or dehydration. It is best to start with small amounts and gradually increase the dosage if necessary.

Section 3: Herbs for Supporting Healthy Digestion and Absorption of Nutrients

1. **Turmeric (Curcuma longa)**

   o **Benefits:** Turmeric is a powerful anti-inflammatory herb that supports digestive health by reducing inflammation in the gut. It contains curcumin, a compound known for its ability to promote bile production, which helps break down fats and improve digestion. Turmeric is also beneficial for individuals with inflammatory bowel conditions like IBS or Crohn's disease.

   o **Use:** Turmeric can be consumed in cooking, teas, or as a supplement. It is often paired with black pepper to enhance its absorption. A warm cup of turmeric tea or golden milk (a blend of turmeric, milk, and honey) can support digestion.

2. **Dandelion (Taraxacum officinale)**

   o **Benefits:** Dandelion is a mild diuretic that helps cleanse the liver and promote bile production. It is commonly used to stimulate appetite and improve digestion. Dandelion also acts as gentle tonic for the digestive system, enhancing nutrient absorption and reducing bloating.

- o **Use:** Dandelion can be consumed as tea, or fresh leaves can be added to salads. Dandelion root is often used in tinctures and capsules for its digestive benefits.

3. **Slippery Elm (Ulmus rubra)**

- o **Benefits:** Slippery elm is known for its soothing effects on the digestive tract. It contains mucilage, a gel-like substance that coats the stomach and intestines, providing relief from irritation, acid reflux, and ulcers. Slippery elm is particularly helpful for individuals with sensitive stomachs or digestive disorders like IBS.

- o **Use:** Slippery elm is commonly consumed as a powder, which can be mixed with water to form a soothing drink. It is also available in capsules and lozenges.

4. **Marshmallow Root (Althaea officinalis)**

- o **Benefits:** Marshmallow root has soothing properties similar to slippery elm. It helps reduce inflammation in the digestive tract and promotes healing of the mucosal lining. Marshmallow root is also used to alleviate heartburn and acid reflux.

- o **Use:** Marshmallow root is available in powder, capsule, or tea form. It can be taken before meals to support digestion and reduce stomach irritation.

Section 4: Herbs for Combating Acid Reflux and Heartburn

1. **Licorice Root (Glycyrrhiza glabra)**

   - o **Benefits:** Licorice root is commonly used to soothe heartburn and acid reflux. It helps protect the mucosal lining of the stomach and esophagus by increasing mucus production. Licorice root also has anti-inflammatory properties that can reduce irritation from acid reflux.

   - o **Use:** Licorice root is typically consumed in the form of tea, tablets, or tincture. It should be used cautiously, as prolonged use can lead to high blood pressure. Deglycyrrhizinated licorice (DGL) is a safer option for long-term use.

2. **Slippery Elm (Ulmus rubra)**

   - o **Benefits:** As mentioned earlier, slippery elm coats and soothes the digestive tract. It provides relief from heartburn and acid reflux by creating a protective barrier in the stomach and esophagus.

- ○ **Use:** Slippery elm powder can be mixed with water and consumed to relieve symptoms of acid reflux or heartburn. It is often used in combination with other herbs for maximum effectiveness.

Conclusion: Nurturing Digestive Health with Herbal Remedies

Herbal remedies offer a natural, gentle, and effective way to support digestive health. Whether you are seeking relief from indigestion, constipation, acid reflux, or simply looking to improve overall gut function, nature provides a wealth of herbs to support your needs. Incorporating these herbs into your daily routine can promote digestive comfort, improve nutrient absorption, and enhance overall well-being

Chapter 16: Herbal Remedies for Skin Health – Natural Solutions for Radiant Skin

Introduction: The Skin as a Reflection of Internal Health

The skin is not only the body's largest organ but also one of the most visible. It acts as a barrier against environmental toxins, microorganisms, and harmful UV radiation while regulating body temperature and maintaining hydration. A healthy, glowing complexion often reflects the body's overall health, while common skin issues like acne, eczema, rosacea, and aging can signal underlying imbalances or stressors.

Herbs have long been used in traditional medicine to support skin health due to their anti-inflammatory, antioxidant, antibacterial, and healing properties. Whether used topically or consumed internally, many herbs can help treat skin conditions, enhance skin tone, and promote youthful, healthy skin.

In this chapter, we will explore herbal remedies for common skin issues, focusing on their healing properties, how to use them, and how they contribute to a natural skincare regimen.

Section 1: Herbs for Promoting Healthy, Radiant Skin

1. **Aloe Vera (Aloe barbadensis)**

   o **Benefits:** Aloe vera is renowned for its soothing and healing properties, particularly for treating burns, cuts, and other skin irritations. It has anti-inflammatory and antioxidant effects that promote skin regeneration, reduce redness, and hydrate the skin. Aloe vera helps maintain skin moisture and prevents dryness, making it a popular remedy for sensitive skin.

   o **Use:** Aloe vera gel can be applied directly to the skin, especially after sun exposure or minor burns. It is also available in creams, lotions, and supplements that promote skin health from the inside out.

2. **Calendula (Calendula officinalis)**

   o **Benefits:** Calendula, or marigold, is known for its ability to heal wounds and soothe irritated skin. It has anti-inflammatory, antibacterial, and antifungal properties, making it effective for treating acne, eczema, and rashes. Calendula is also useful in promoting collagen production, helping to maintain youthful and healthy skin.

   o **Use:** Calendula can be used in creams, ointments, or oils for topical application. It can also be infused into teas to improve skin health internally.

3. **Lavender (Lavandula angustifolia)**

   o **Benefits:** Lavender is well-known for its calming and anti-inflammatory properties. It can help soothe irritated or inflamed skin and is often used to treat conditions such as acne, eczema, and psoriasis. Lavender also has antibacterial properties, which can help prevent skin infections and acne outbreaks. Additionally, its antioxidant content helps protect the skin from premature aging.

   o **Use:** Lavender essential oil can be diluted and applied to the skin for localized treatment of acne or eczema. It can also be added to bathwater for a soothing, relaxing experience.

4. **Rosemary (Rosmarinus officinalis)**

   o **Benefits:** Rosemary has antioxidant and anti inflammatory properties, making it an excellent herb for improving skin tone and texture. I helps stimulate blood circulation, promoting the regeneration of skin cells and reducing the appearance of wrinkles and fine lines Rosemary is also effective in reducing puffiness and dark circles around the eyes.

   o **Use:** Rosemary oil can be used in face masks added to skincare products, or massaged into the skin to stimulate circulation and rejuvenate the complexion. It can also be taken internally as a tea to improve skin health from the inside out.

5. **Chamomile (Matricaria chamomilla)**

   - **Benefits:** Chamomile is a gentle yet effective herb for soothing skin irritation, redness, and inflammation. It is commonly used to treat conditions like eczema, acne, and rosacea. Chamomile's calming properties make it ideal for sensitive or inflamed skin, providing relief from itching and irritation. It also has antioxidant benefits that support skin repair and reduce signs of aging.

   - **Use:** Chamomile tea can be used both internally and topically. The tea can be applied to the skin using a cotton ball to calm irritation or promote healing. Chamomile oil or cream can also be applied directly to affected areas.

Section 2: Herbs for Treating Specific Skin Conditions

1. **Neem (Azadirachta indica)**

   - **Benefits:** Neem is a powerful herb with antibacterial, antifungal, and antiviral properties, making it an excellent remedy for acne and other skin infections. It also helps reduce inflammation and redness while promoting the healing of scars and blemishes. Neem's detoxifying effects help purify the blood, which can lead to clearer skin over time.

- o **Use:** Neem oil can be applied directly to acne spots or used as a face mask to treat acne. Neem powder or leaves can also be used to make a paste for applying to the skin or for inclusion in a bath soak.

2. **Witch Hazel (Hamamelis virginiana)**

- o **Benefits:** Witch hazel is an astringent herb that helps tone the skin, tighten pores, and reduce excess oil. It is commonly used to treat acne, blackheads, and oily skin. Witch hazel also has anti-inflammatory properties that help calm irritated skin and reduce swelling or redness.

- o **Use:** Witch hazel can be applied directly to the skin using a cotton pad, especially on areas prone to acne or oiliness. It is available in various toners and skincare products designed for acne-prone or oily skin.

3. **Tea Tree Oil (Melaleuca alternifolia)**

- o **Benefits:** Tea tree oil is a well-known antibacterial and antifungal herb that helps fight acne, fungal infections, and other skin conditions. It is particularly effective in reducing the inflammation and infection associated with acne and pimples. Tea tree oil also helps regulate oil production, preventing clogged pores that lead to breakouts.

- ○ **Use:** Tea tree oil should always be diluted with a carrier oil (like coconut or jojoba oil) before being applied to the skin. It can be used as a spot treatment for acne or added to face masks and cleansers for regular use.

4. **Comfrey (Symphytum officinale)**

- ○ **Benefits:** Comfrey has been used for centuries to promote wound healing and tissue repair. It is often used to treat cuts, bruises, and scars. Comfrey contains allantoin, a compound that promotes the regeneration of skin cells, helping to heal wounds and reduce scarring.

- ○ **Use:** Comfrey can be applied topically as an ointment or cream to help speed up the healing process of wounds or burns. It should not be used on broken skin or deep wounds without professional guidance, as it can sometimes cause irritation.

Section 3: Herbs for Anti-Aging and Wrinkle Prevention

1. **Ginseng (Panax ginseng)**

- ○ **Benefits:** Ginseng is a powerful adaptogen with antioxidant properties that help fight free radicals, which contribute to the aging process. It promotes collagen production, improving skin elasticity and reducing the appearance of fine lines and wrinkles. Ginseng also supports blood circulation, ensuring that the skin receives adequate nutrients and oxygen.

- o **Use:** Ginseng can be taken as a supplement, in teas, or applied topically in creams or serums to rejuvenate the skin and prevent premature aging.

2. **Gotu Kola (Centella Asiatica)**

- o **Benefits:** Gotu kola is known for its ability to stimulate collagen production and improve skin elasticity. It has anti-aging properties that help reduce the appearance of fine lines and wrinkles and promote overall skin rejuvenation. Gotu kola also supports the healing of scars and stretch marks by enhancing the production of connective tissue.

- o **Use:** Gotu kola can be applied in skincare products or taken internally as a supplement to support collagen synthesis and promote youthful skin.

3. **Hibiscus (Hibiscus sabdariffa)**

- o **Benefits:** Hibiscus is a natural source of alpha hydroxy acids (AHAs), which are commonly used in skincare products to exfoliate the skin and promote cell turnover. It helps reduce wrinkles, fine lines, and age spots by gently sloughing off dead skin cells and revealing smoother, more youthful skin.

- ○ **Use:** Hibiscus tea can be consumed for its antioxidant benefits, or the flower extract can be found in various anti-aging creams, masks, and serums.

Conclusion: Embracing Nature's Wisdom for Healthy Skin

Herbal remedies provide a natural, effective way to support skin health, from soothing irritation and treating acne to preventing aging and promoting radiant skin. By incorporating these powerful plants into your skincare routine, you can enhance your skin's appearance and address specific skin concerns in a gentle, holistic manner. Whether you choose to apply herbs topically or consume them internally, these natural remedies offer a wealth of benefits for your skin's health, beauty, and vitality.

As with any natural remedy, it's important to do a patch test before applying new herbs to your skin, especially if you have sensitive skin or allergies. For chronic or severe skin conditions, consult a healthcare provider to ensure that herbal treatments complement your overall wellness plan.

Made in the USA
Las Vegas, NV
12 December 2024

14019227R00085